Earn A
Second Income
From Your
Woodworking

Garth Graves

BETTERWAY BOOKS
CINCINNATI, OHIO

ABOUT THE AUTHOR

Garth Graves has been a woodworker for thirty-six years, designing and producing projects for his home, boat and for woodworking publications. He is the author/illustrator of *Desks You Can Customize*, *Woodworker's Guide to Furniture Design* and *Yacht Craftsman's Handbook*. He is also a contributor to *Woodenboat*, *Classic Boat*, *Fine Woodworking*, *Popular Woodworking* and *Better Homes and Gardens* magazines.

Earn a Second Income From Your Woodworking. Copyright © 1997 by Garth Graves. Printed and bound in the United States of America. All rights reserved. No part of this book may be reproduced in any form or by any electronic or mechanical means including information storage and retrieval systems without permission in writing from the publisher, except by a reviewer, who may quote brief passages in a review. Published by Betterway Books, an imprint of F&W Publications, Inc., 1507 Dana Avenue, Cincinnati, Ohio 45207. (800) 289-0963. First edition.

Other fine Betterway Books are available from your local bookstore or direct from the publisher.

01 00 99 98 97   5 4 3 2 1

Library of Congress Cataloging-in-Publication Data

Graves, Garth.
    Earn a second income from your woodworking / by Garth Graves.
       p.   cm.
    Includes index.
    ISBN 1-55870-464-7 (alk. paper)
    1. Woodworking industries—Management. 2. New business enterprises—Management. 3. Woodwork—Marketing. I. Title.
HD9773.A2G7   1997
684′.08′068—dc21

97-25910
CIP

Edited by Bruce E. Stoker
Production Edited by Michelle Kramer
Interior designed by Pamela Koenig
Cover designed by Stephanie Redman
Cover photo by Hal Barkan, BKT Photography

Special thanks to Cliff Wagner and the Workshops of the Restoration Society, Inc. in Latonia, Kentucky.

Betterway Books are available for sales promotions, premiums and fund-raising use. Special editions or book excerpts can also be created to specification. For details contact: Special Sales Manager, F&W Publications, 1507 Dana Avenue, Cincinnati, Ohio 45207.

METRIC CONVERSION CHART

to convert	to	multiply by
Inches	Centimeters	2.54
Centimeters	Inches	0.4
Feet	Centimeters	30.5
Centimeters	Feet	0.03
Yards	Meters	0.9
Meters	Yards	1.1
Sq. Inches	Sq. Centimeters	6.45
Sq. Centimeters	Sq. Inches	0.16
Sq. Feet	Sq. Meters	0.09
Sq. Meters	Sq. Feet	10.8
Sq. Yards	Sq. Meters	0.8
Sq. Meters	Sq. Yards	1.2
Pounds	Kilograms	0.45
Kilograms	Pounds	2.2
Ounces	Grams	28.4
Grams	Ounces	0.04

ACKNOWLEDGMENTS

First, thank you to the artisans/craftspeople who enthusiastically shared their time, talent and experiences for the profiles presented throughout this book:

Mark Allen—Dana Point, California

Randy Bader—Laguna Beach, California

Dean Douglas—Albuquerque, New Mexico

Michael Dunbar—Hampton, New Hampshire

Michael Elkan—Silverton, Oregon

David Lomas/Debra Doucette—Wakefield, Massachusetts

Salvatore Maccarone—Port Townsend, Washington

Carol Reed—Ramona, California

Jon Sauer—Pacifica, California

Jennifer Schwarz—Port Townsend, Washington

Jonathan Simons—Kempton, Pennsylvania

Charles Shackleton—Bridgewater, Vermont

Bob Stevenson—Chula Vista, California

Tom Stockton—Petaluma, California

Myron Van Ness—Laguna Beach, California

Also to the scores of woodworkers who were recommended by various sources, but not contacted. Their stories and approaches to the woodworking business were known to gallery operators, show organizers, magazine editors and woodworking suppliers. This group is obviously doing a good job promoting themselves but go unnamed here due only to a lack of space and no reflection on their accomplishments. All would have a story to tell.

Among the sources helpful in passing on their enthusiasm for the craft, and naming some people plying it, include:

Paul Anthony, *American Woodworker Magazine*

Adam Blake, Editor, Betterway Books

Ian Bowen, Editor, *Woodshop News*

Christopher Brooks, Northwest Fine Woodworking, Seattle, WA

Lammont Copeland, Jr., Publisher, *The Crafts Report*

Ron Goldman, *Woodworker West Magazine*

Kingsley Hammett, Sante Fe, NM

Matt Higgens, Woodworkers Supply of New Mexico

Peggy Kutcher, North Bennet Street School, Boston, MA

Scott LaFlam, Woodworker's Store, San Diego, CA

Albert LeCoff, Woodturning Center, Inc. Philadelphia, PA

Tony Lydgate, Publisher, *Professional Craft Journal*

Wendy Rosen, The Rosen Group, Baltimore, MD

David Sloan, Publisher, *American Woodworker Magazine*

Jim Tolpin, Port Townsend, WA

Julie Turley, American Craft Council

Paul Zurowski, Sawbridge Studios, Chicago, IL

TABLE OF CONTENTS

CHAPTER

6

HOW DO I MAKE AND KEEP MY BUSINESS PROFITABLE?   82

CHAPTER

7

HOW DO I PRICE AND SELL MY WORK?   96

CHAPTER

8

HOW DO I GROW MY BUSINESS?   112

INTRODUCTION

The one key to success is . . .

If only we could finish that sentence, we could all be rich and famous.

But there are different keys to success, as shown throughout *Earn a Second Income From Your Woodworking*. Different needs, abilities, interests and approaches, applied either singularly or in combination, lead to success on different paths, at different rates.

The case studies of part- and full-time artisans profiled in this book—all earning income in woodworking—are studies in contrast, with both shared and opposing views on how *the business of woodworking* should be approached and what you should expect from your efforts. While the majority of these craftspeople entered the business full time, they exhibit the income potential of your part-time venture—the carrot, the brass ring.

APPROACH

The profiles offer a closer look at how these artisans go about meeting their own objectives, whether earning a living or supplementing other income. You will gain an understanding of how they started and what they've achieved by relying on their own agenda, developed out of their personal make-up, ambition, confidence and ability. Their individual approaches to the business make their unique combination of product/production/marketing successful.

DIVERSITY

This is a widely diverse group of woodworkers. Some are self-taught and some are schooled in the crafts, some are business-driven and others are driven by the craft they produce. Some have a strong art background while others come from the trades or a hobby. Some sell only direct at the retail level and some sell at wholesale only, appreciative of the sales assistance and client screening offered by galleries and promoters. Some do shows and some do not. . . . They're all making money.

NICHE KNACK AND ATTITUDE

There are three attributes they all share. One is a niche, a product they know well, and have a high level of expertise in producing. Secondly, they all have a knack for finding the right niche marketplace. The third is a positive attitude. Even with some occasional doubts, they all share the ability to communicate a confidence in themselves and in their products.

SELF-PPROMOTION

A product can be excellent but you have to sell yourself with it—it comes as a package. Customers, and especailly gallery buyers, buy into what you represent as well as what you produce.

There are different keys to success and no one key for all. Hopefully the profiles cover enough disciplines, outlooks, products and approaches to enable you to be better prepared on your road to success in the business of woodworking.

1

HOW MUCH CAN I MAKE?

Success is relative. At the risk of answering a question with a question—how much do you want to make? It is far simpler to keep it simple at the beginning, and maybe for all time, if "simple" fits your objectives and desired level of commitment to the business. Your objectives may be:

- to supplement your salary or retirement income
- to recover the direct and indirect costs of your woodworking activity—to pay for the time and materials for doing what you enjoy
- to supplement your income over and above the cost of doing business—a profit motive
- to launch into a full-blown full-time woodworking business

At any of these levels, a commitment to the venture is crucial. Commitment is discussed repeatedly throughout this book. Among other things, it includes:

- the time you are willing to commit to the business
- the resources, both available and obtainable, you can commit for tools, equipment and shop space
- a willingness to do your least-favorite tasks (marketing, selling, accounting, collecting) instead of what you would rather be doing in the shop
- a balance of commitment between business and family

Demands on your time and resources will grow as your business grows, as you discover firsthand what is working and what is not, and your time will be stretched in a number of areas. Where you apply your own time should be based on what you personally bring to the business and where you can best apply your special skills and interest. Fine craftsmanship is labor-intensive. Someday you may consider hiring a helper in the shop or a representative in the field, or pushing more paperwork off on your accountant so you can, once again, spend time creating and producing.

Whether in a second income start-up, or making the move from part- to full-time, you will be doing it all. Some forms of assistance and lots of support are available through co-ops, guilds and apprenticeship programs. Many craftspeople establish a loose "partnership," maybe by sharing shop space and shop equipment with another artisan of similar or complementing skills. They can share the rent and help each other when there is a lull in their own work. In-kind support, such as helping your cabinetmaker counterpart when he is busy, can be returned when you have a job that takes over the shop.

A one-person shop is probably the most manageable structure for a business. From the customer's standpoint, that one person's piece of furniture sold directly to the consumer has added value. The qualities the artisan brings to the work—design excellence, meticulous joinery, attention to detail and fine finishes—can be theirs at the same price they would pay for a comparable commercial piece at a retail furniture store, where half the cost to the consumer goes into marketing and sales.

If you build it well and price it fairly, for both yourself and your customers, they will opt for the added value they receive from your product.

The majority of artisans profiled in this book prefer to work solo. Randy Bader's views on the subject are clear. To paraphrase his interview presented in chapter five, he cautions would-be employers about:

1. doing the work if worker doesn't show up

2. trying to explain what you do when you design on the fly

3. finding "busywork" between operations or during production lags

4. watching someone else work at a slower pace without the owner's level of care and appreciation for quality

5. opening the flow of regulatory responsibilities as an employer

As a start-up company, you may not be able to add helpers to the workforce, but as your business grows there might be a need for production or administrative assistance that must be jobbed out to others. Just when that will occur in your growth and when it will be time to talk about the specifics, will come later, as does more discussion on the subject in chapter three.

Do you want or need to mass-produce, or will your product(s) support one-of-a-kind pricing with adequate profit margins? The key here is: How many widgets can you make and sell, and still enjoy it?

IS YOUR IDEA FEASIBLE?

Will what you make, or plan to make, keep you in the manner you would like to be accustomed? Within the time you have allocated to woodworking, can you produce and sell enough units to realize a respectable return on your invested time and cash resources?

One observation that comes from nearly every sector of business supporting the woodcraft trade—suppliers, promoters, retailers, publishers—is you need to find a niche and exploit it if you are to have a chance at success. If you follow the flock and compete with the run-of-the-mill crowd, it will be far more difficult to prosper. More than likely there are craftsmen out there who do it better and cheaper. If your work is simply on par with this group, they have the advantage

of a head start with a marketing pipeline, which can take years to develop, in place and flowing.

WHAT LEVEL OF INCOME CAN YOU EXPECT?

What you make and where you sell it will obviously govern how much income you can realistically expect from the business. A single item, whether built on commission or on speculation, sold directly to the buyer maximizes the net gain from your own craftsmanship and sales efforts. A few big-ticket, high-end items per year, such as a commission to produce a roomful or houseful of custom furniture, can keep your one-person shop humming.

Smaller products may mean a larger customer base. You don't have the time yourself to both produce the goods and prospect the customers, so if the product is a good fit for a show, fair or festival, you can share a little of the gross income to rent a booth, pay your entry fee and spend some traveling money to hawk your products at the show. This approach concentrates your sales and marketing efforts on prequalified prospective buyers drawn to the event through their interests, and to your booth by the product you are showcasing. You should price the item to cover cost of goods and expenses plus whatever markup the value of the item will command.

Markets to consider

" . . . we did almost every craft show that came along. For two years running, we showed a lot, and that turned out to be too much work. I have slowly reduced it to where I do one show a year—one Christmas show in November. That's all I can really handle. My time is really filled. I have to be careful about what I'm getting into because I'm looking ahead for a whole year."—Dean Douglas (see profile in chapter six)

At times you will find a particular format of an event is a perfect match between product and buyer.

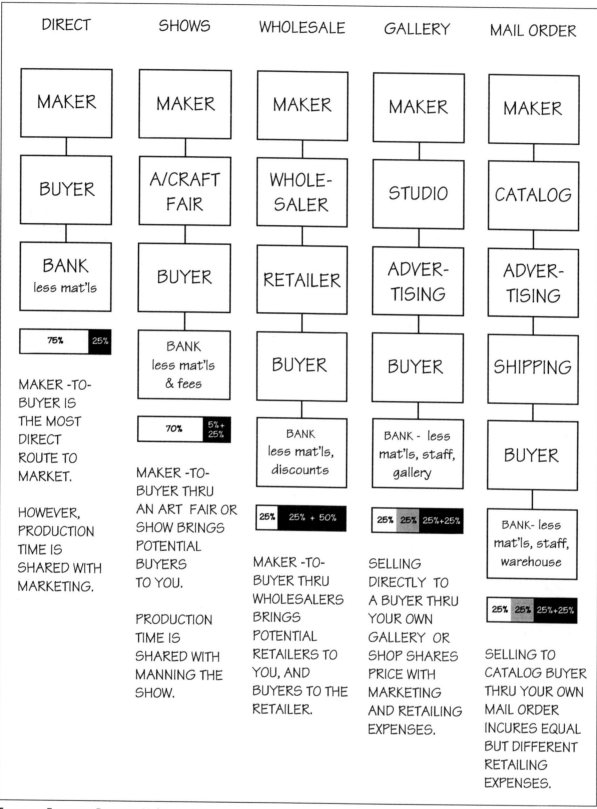

DIRECT

MAKER

BUYER

BANK
less mat'ls

| 75% | 25% |

MAKER-TO-BUYER IS THE MOST DIRECT ROUTE TO MARKET.

HOWEVER, PRODUCTION TIME IS SHARED WITH MARKETING.

SHOWS

MAKER

A/CRAFT FAIR

BUYER

BANK
less mat'ls & fees

| 70% | 5%+ 25% |

MAKER-TO-BUYER THRU AN ART FAIR OR SHOW BRINGS POTENTIAL BUYERS TO YOU.

PRODUCTION TIME IS SHARED WITH MANNING THE SHOW.

WHOLESALE

MAKER

WHOLE-SALER

RETAILER

BUYER

BANK
less mat'ls, discounts

| 25% | 25% + 50% |

MAKER-TO-BUYER THRU WHOLESALERS BRINGS POTENTIAL RETAILERS TO YOU, AND BUYERS TO THE RETAILER.

GALLERY

MAKER

STUDIO

ADVER-TISING

BUYER

BANK - less mat'ls, staff, gallery

| 25% | 25% | 25%+25% |

SELLING DIRECTLY TO A BUYER THRU YOUR OWN GALLERY OR SHOP SHARES PRICE WITH MARKETING AND RETAILING EXPENSES.

MAIL ORDER

MAKER

CATALOG

ADVER-TISING

SHIPPING

BUYER

BANK- less mat'ls, staff, warehouse

| 25% | 25% | 25%+25% |

SELLING TO CATALOG BUYER THRU YOUR OWN MAIL ORDER INCURES EQUAL BUT DIFFERENT RETAILING EXPENSES.

FIGURE 1-1 Expenses Between Maker and Buyer

If the show nets all the work you can handle, look no further.

As the figure columns on page 10 read from left to right, more resources (and expenses) are applied to bringing your product to market, and, obviously, you net less on each piece. You must adjust pricing and volume upward to cover the added costs.

Custom or limited production premium items are candidates that may sell to high-end buyers through galleries—people in the trade.

Sales commissions

Selling your wares through galleries that attract ready and able buyers of your item can reduce your potential return by 40 to 50 percent. This might be a good investment if your product is well represented and presented in a setting that really showcases your work among other complementing pieces, in a location and showroom that caters to the level of buyer your craftsmanship commands.

This pricing level works only if you can produce and price your pieces to net your desired profit margin at the wholesale level and if the value commands a premium markup to cover the gallery's or retailer's expense and profit margin.

By operating your own studio/gallery, your net income (what is left after all the expenses are reduced from the gross selling price) will be reduced by the costs to attract buyers and operate a small gallery that would otherwise be borne by the outside retailer, but the profit realized by the retailer will be yours instead of theirs.

People are in business to profit from their activities. Even if you plan to work on referral only, there may be some commissions associated with this source of sales. A friend telling a friend is usually free. However, an architect or interior designer may be thinking referral fee, and most likely any work that is obtained through any sort of gallery representation will command some referral fee. This could be the same 40 to 50 percent for a piece sold from the gallery floor, or it could be a 10 to 20 percent referral fee if the business was obtained through the gallery's marketing efforts. Be alert to that possibility and be ready to negotiate a fee for their involvement. Sometimes you don't know the source of the referral. Referral fees should be recouped in your price.

You can operate your personal scaled-down gallery by designating an area of your workshop/studio as a showroom, either at the outset, if you have the space, or when you plan your expanded facility. Some items show best in an upscale sales environment, but there is also some benefit in showing the client the piece as well as where and how you produce it, which would be an argument for showing at your workshop.

A mail-order business, if that is in your plans, will require a like amount of sales expense as a walk-in gallery, except the money otherwise spent on operating a retail location will shift to pay for your catalog, advertising, warehousing, direct mail and other costs associated with the mail-order business. Volume production is a prerequisite for this form of marketing.

So when considering what level of income you can expect, first reach some conclusion on how you will market the product. Chapter seven contains thoughts and guidelines on pricing your work, and the following will help you decide what to build, how many, where to sell them and at what cost.

Balancing costs and price

Consider the balance of production cost to product value, or the price the piece will command.

Success comes from a balance of product and pricing. The two parts of the equation are (1) your cost of producing value in a piece that will (2) command the price from the buyer. When first developing the product or idea, the balance may be heavily weighed on the cost of production. To attain, maintain or regain a product that will command a price may mean adjusting your ways. Look at reducing costs through production efficiencies and buying smarter, and increasing value to get higher-end results by enhancing the design, the materials and the craftsmanship. If you have done everything right and are at maximum efficiency, look at

Profits come from a balance between:

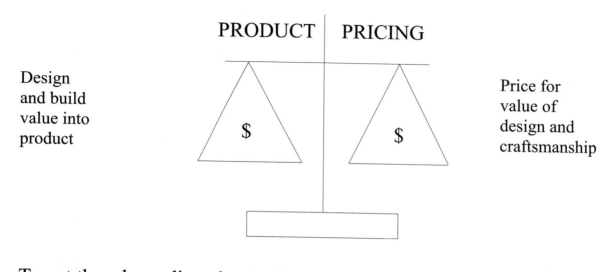

PRODUCT | PRICING

Design
and build
value into
product

$

$

Price for
value of
design and
craftsmanship

To get the edge, adjust the product ...

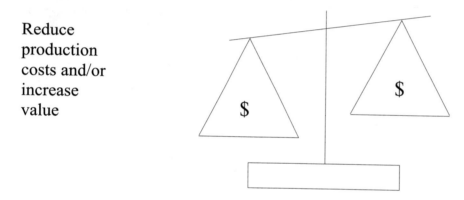

Reduce
production
costs and/or
increase
value

$

$

At max value added, study your market ...

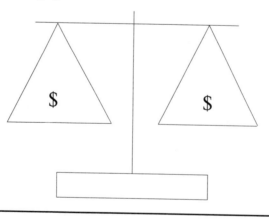

$

$

Look at where
you are selling.
Go up-scale,
increase price,
increase volume,
reduce sales
costs

FIGURE 1-2 Adjusting the Costs

the marketing side and try to increase price, and/or increase volume or reduce sales costs to net the maximum return from your product.

WHAT INCOME LEVEL DO YOU NEED?

Woodworking for a second income can supplement the coffers, but by how much depends on what you make and how many times you want to make and sell it. Also, the route you take to market will determine what return you can realize—how much you can keep.

When moving from a part- to full-time business, choosing the road to market becomes even more critical. Positive net income is a must, not a want. Cash flow from a single source of income is critical to meeting both your operating and living expenses.

There are more questions you should ask to determine the income you need. Answers will differ for each reader. Hopefully there are examples throughout this book that are right on, or at least close to your personal scenario. But for now, consider:

- Do you want to cover expenses of materials, make some extra money from your hobby, start a retirement business or launch into a full-time venture?
- What other income stream are you working from?
- How long will this continue?
- Can all living expenses be covered by the woodworking effort?
- How much start-up time can you afford?

Health care concerns

Issues for the self-employed to consider include things like health care premiums. If you are currently among the ranks of the employed, you've noticed the employee's share of health care insurance has been on the rise. Private coverage is expensive, sometimes reaching $10,000 a year. Leaving a plan at work, you can continue your insurance coverage under the COBRA (Consolidated Omnibus Budget Reconcilliation Act) plan, and you pay the employer's share. This lasts 18 months, at which time you would need private coverage.

Tax concerns

Tax laws are changing in favor of the self-employed. As of this writing, 30 percent of the health insurance premiums are deductible from income tax. This limit was recently amended to include an expanding scale for deductibility. Check with your accountant for the specifics, but even with some tax relief, these costs are included in the cost of doing business.

Benefit concerns

If you are still employed, or your spouse is employed and receives employee benefits, the full burden of this expense is not on the woodworking business. If you have reached the age where Medicare kicks in, you don't have the level of concerns as do those without these benefits. There are some options to consider. The American Craft Council represents a "group" of professional craftspeople and shop owners in the crafts. Also, the American Association of Retired Persons (AARP) recently announced the availability of group coverage for persons over age 50 but not yet eligible for Social Security and Medicare.

IS YOUR PRODUCT NOVEL— WHAT IS YOUR NICHE?

Here, novel doesn't necessarily mean different—just a twist or a plus that other similar products lack. This could just as easily be something ultratraditional in a market that leans toward being trendy.

Novel can be producing what is in vogue at any point in time, in a specific locale. Buyers look for quality Shaker furniture in Shaker country, Southwestern style from the Southwest. All styles at or near their points of origin draw a clientele.

Chic today may be Windsor or Stickley, with origins in sometimes crude, utilitarian furniture that was an alternative to ultra-ornate furniture of times past. Today these styles have been elevated to high-quality, well-crafted designs for an elite market.

The niche you are not looking for would be to follow the mass-production crowd to market with a product that is saturated with low-cost goods. Chapter four contains a survey of what items galleries are selling most. These can be an indication of need, but while filling that need, look to the next trend.

Once again, the answer to the question, "Is my product novel?" may be a list of questions:

1. Do your product and marketing approach have a hook? Is there something distinctive that grabs the prospective client?

NAME: **David Lomas and Debra Doucette, d/b/a D+D Woodworking**

LOCATION: **Wakefield, Massachusetts**

PRODUCT: **Turned pen/pencil sets. Scroll saw work. Wooden percussion instruments.**

SINCE: **1994**

TRAINING: **Self-taught**

SHOP: **Basement workshop**

PRICING: **Currently retail. Objective is wholesale.**

AFFILIATIONS: **Shows at street fairs and festivals. Manufacturing wooden percussion symphony instruments. Talking with merchants in Fannuel Hall, Boston, Massachusetts.**

David Lomas and Debra Doucette have teamed up in life and in their new part-time business, D+D Woodworking in Wakefield, Massachusetts. David is producing turned pens and pencils, and Debra is into scroll saw products. They are pleased with making a little money from craft shows and have become manufacturers of wooden percussion instruments by watching for opportunities.

Q How did you get started in the woodworking business?

A We started out looking for a hobby. Five years ago we were in Sears one night looking at the routers and Deb said, "That looks like fun," and we bought one, and it mushroomed from there. At that time we just started buying tools and equipment, and the more tools we bought, the more we did, and the more we did, the more we needed. I never really thought about doing anything in woodworking for an income. It was just a hobby, and it became a very serious hobby. And then Deb got a scroll saw and it started mushrooming from there. She started making all these small items and we thought that maybe we could do a craft fair with all the stuff we had in inventory and it would be a way, if nothing else, just to kind of support our hobbies. If we made any money from the craft fair, that was good. We could go buy some more wood or some more scroll saw blades.

Q What was the most valuable skill or attribute you brought to the venture?

A The most valuable attribute would be our basic mechanical abilities. Both of us. She had as much mechanical ability as I had. Very self-sufficient. Deb is very logical in her thinking.

Q What was the major obstacle you encountered?

A I expected to be better at woodworking sooner. Deb has more patience with that. I was just reading a book the other night, a book of projects and plans from Jointech. In the introduction of the book, the author said that he had been at it for forty years (and I for only five) and he considered himself as still learning.

Self-promotion and pricing remain obstacles. Neither of us can promote ourself. For those with more of a business background, that may be easy; for us that aspect is a struggle.

Q What are your plans for growth?

A We would like to increase product line. The musical contract will move with us when we relocate to the seashore, but we want to expand into products that will go over with the tourist trade at the seaport resort. And Deb would like to create a book of scroll saw plans someday.

Q The first local show was a small show?

A Our first show, about a year ago, was a small fund-raiser for the Wakefield Music Boosters for the local high school band. We did very well for us. We really went in with no expectations at all and came out with $180. I took my lathe with me and demonstrated my pen and pencil turning. And it drew customers.

Q Can you see any difference in buyer interest when you don't demo?

A The one show that I did the demos, we did well. The shows after that where I didn't do the demos, we did very poorly. Now, I can't attribute that to not demonstrating, but it helps. Any time we do a craft show again I am going to try to do demonstrations. We plan to demo both the small lathe turning and scroll saw work, alternating an hour each.

Q Are you into retail outlets?

A We have talked to some retailers. There is one in Boston and he wants to see some of our wares. We haven't had the time, but one of our goals would be to get our merchandise out into the retail market.

We are not salespeople. We would rather make the stuff and let somebody else sell it—ship 20 or 30 to 100 of something to one store and let them deal with it. That would be our ultimate goal.

There is a place in Boston called Fannuel Hall, and this fellow sells all kinds of higher quality handmade wood products from a vendor cart—little boxes. I think Deb's scrollwork shelves and brackets, and I definitely think my pens and pencils would go over well.

Q How did you make contact?

A We were just visiting and saw his operation. Deb and I went over and started talking. You never know.

We may move to Delaware next year, where I'm from originally. It is down near the southern end of the state near a town called Rehoboth Beach, a resort area, and as in any resort area there are a lot of craft stores, and we hope to get into some of them.

We also do musical instruments. We were in a woodworker's store, Woodcraft, where Deb saw a little ad on the bulletin board. Some company was looking for woodworkers with a belt sander, a drill press and a router to do some work.

We didn't know what kind of work it was, so we called them, sent them a resume and business card. Three weeks later we got a call and met with them. The man who owns the percussion instrument company is a percussionist for the Boston Symphony Orchestra, among others, and sells to orchestras throughout the world. He makes drums, tambourines, drumsticks, timpani mallets, gong mallets and wood blocks.

The first product he wanted us to manufacture for him were the wood blocks. We discussed it for a while, went home and made a sample and took it back and he liked it, so ever since then we have been woodworking for him. We just finished a $650 week for him.

Q You're just making blocks?

A His product line has mushroomed since we started with the blocks. We make his timpani mallets and gong mallets. That wasn't part of the original contract, but he liked our work and he has given us that. He also makes clips, almost like a clothespin, only fancier, to hold the triangles to a music stand. The clips are made from leftover maple we use to make the blocks, and there is a lot of it leftover, paid for and we have it. From that we've made these clips, handles for various instruments. What I'm saying is that is all free materials, because the wood is already bought and paid for in the block project, and we turn it around and make the clips.

Q How would you rank quality, craftsmanship, design and price in their order of importance?

A Quality is number one. They all are number one. The design is very important, craftsmanship is quality, and of course you want to make a fair amount of money out of it.

We've found as far as pricing—my father always said his family couldn't sell a dime for a nickel—we're just not sales-minded people. At the craft shows, we would rather price something for less and sell it than try to get more money out of something and take a chance of not selling it.

A fellow came up to our booth at one craft show and said, "I wouldn't sell this piece for less than $75." The point was we weren't selling it for $40; why would we want to not sell it for $75? We would rather sell it for $40 or $30 without being insulted than to try to get an outrageous price from something. I would have to say that price is a little less important. We would rather just sell it than make a bundle.

It will take a while. We've only been doing the selling part of it for about a year.

---

2. Does your product fill a need—aesthetic, function or prestige?

3. Will it sell? At your price? Buyers of wooden items appreciate the beauty of the natural wood and the form and shape in which it is presented. Uniqueness is expected, as is craftsmanship, fine joinery, quality finishes and all else that goes into making your design a reality.

If you are into furniture reproductions or replicas, do your homework and deliver authentic designs, processes and finishes. When contemporizing a style, put more of yourself into the design, but avoid offending prospective buyers by bastardizing the design. If billed as a Shaker-type, the product should have Shaker proportions and details.

In talking to woodworkers for this book, the underlying theme, the thread that ties the case studies presented in this book, is that successful woodworkers have found a niche product that appeals to a buying sector and sells where there is a supporting market base. In other words, the right combination of product-to-market, considering the locale, the demographic profiles of the prospective buyers it draws and the seasonal ebb and flow of the consumers through the shop location.

CAN YOU PRODUCE YOUR PRODUCT COST-EFFECTIVELY?

Regardless of the price you set for your work, a major portion of the selling price goes toward the costs of labor (your time), materials and facilities used to pro-

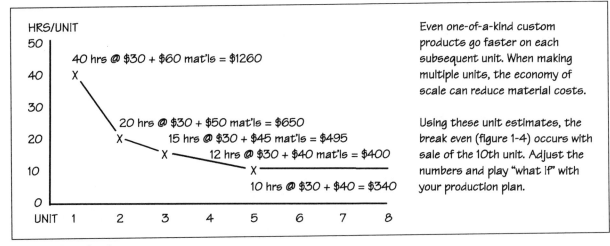

HRS/UNIT

40 hrs @ $30 + $60 mat'ls = $1260

20 hrs @ $30 + $50 mat'ls = $650
15 hrs @ $30 + $45 mat'ls = $495
12 hrs @ $30 + $40 mat'ls = $400

10 hrs @ $30 + $40 = $340

UNIT 1 2 3 4 5 6 7 8

Even one-of-a-kind custom products go faster on each subsequent unit. When making multiple units, the economy of scale can reduce material costs.

Using these unit estimates, the break even (figure 1-4) occurs with sale of the 10th unit. Adjust the numbers and play "what if" with your production plan.

FIGURE 1-3 Learning Curve

duce it. You will need a product that will command the profit margins necessary to sustain your business. Again, this is much more likely to occur only if you market in fruitful fields.

Once you define that magic relationship of product-to-market, and discover what the market will bear, look at how you might become more efficient at what you produce without compromising the level of quality and craftsmanship you want to maintain.

Labor hours required to build one-of-a-kind items will decline, although slightly, with each item. Economy of scale, ganging and grouping of operations and improved methods learned along the way will promote efficiency, even in dissimilar products.

Productivity will improve with the experience gained making the first and subsequent units. When making multiples of the same or similar designs, the time required to complete each successive item will decline with experience. The shop math has been calculated, the jigs and fixtures are fabricated and available for reuse, and you have discovered a better, faster way to make the item. Even when producing custom or art pieces, the bugs will be worked out in the prototype or first article. Similar parts will be ganged, similar operations (even though performed on different designs) will go faster, and materials can be purchased in greater quantities at a better price.

There will come a time in producing an item that

you can't trim any more expense from your production costs without impacting quality. The first item still takes the most time to produce, and if it is the only one made, it must carry the brunt of all design and tooling costs. The learning curve applies in using similar steps, methods and techniques whether the product is a chest or an umbrella stand.

The economy of scale brings down the cost of mass-produced items more quickly than handcrafted products, but there will still be a cross-over of units made and cost per unit.

As quantities increase, each will bear a lesser percentage of the associated costs. There will be a point where the two lines cross, which is when breakeven occurs. The items you produce and sell beyond the break-even point spread your cost of doing business and allow greater financial return from your efforts.

"People said we could never make money handcrafting furniture and selling it wholesale. We do make money ($1.3 million this year), and one of the reasons we do is that I very much enjoy running a business, and I also believe that the only way it would work was by involving people who worked with me."—Charles Shackleton

Mass or even limited production brings the cost per unit down, then crosses over at the break-even point. This applies to one-of-a-kind work as well. Your business

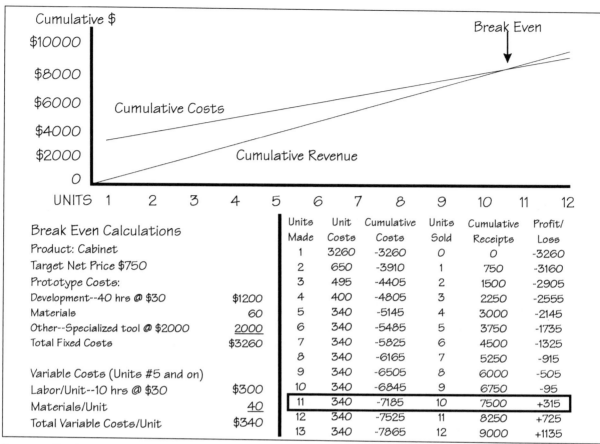

Figure with graph showing Cumulative Costs and Cumulative Revenue lines crossing at Break Even point.

Break Even Calculations

Product: Cabinet

Target Net Price $750

Prototype Costs:	
Development--40 hrs @ $30	$1200
Materials	60
Other--Specialized tool @ $2000	2000
Total Fixed Costs	$3260

Variable Costs (Units #5 and on)	
Labor/Unit--10 hrs @ $30	$300
Materials/Unit	40
Total Variable Costs/Unit	$340

Units Made	Unit Costs	Cumulative Costs	Units Sold	Cumulative Receipts	Profit/ Loss
1	3260	-3260	0	0	-3260
2	650	-3910	1	750	-3160
3	495	-4405	2	1500	-2905
4	400	-4805	3	2250	-2555
5	340	-5145	4	3000	-2145
6	340	-5485	5	3750	-1735
7	340	-5825	6	4500	-1325
8	340	-6165	7	5250	-915
9	340	-6505	8	6000	-505
10	340	-6845	9	6750	-95
11	340	-7185	10	7500	+315
12	340	-7525	11	8250	+725
13	340	-7865	12	9000	+1135

FIGURE 1-4 Breakeven

plan should project this break-even point. Maybe your first few units won't cover costs, but the projected sales quantities will average out at a per-unit profit.

IS THERE DEMAND FOR YOUR PRODUCT?

Demand can be one-piece, one-person, or ten for ten and progressing up from there. Conducting your own market research will provide an indication of demand for your goods.

Compare your product, your product line or your style with consumer demand at the one-of-a-kind, limited production or mass-production levels for a positive indicator to start up. Look at the life expectancy of this popular item or style and determine whether the market is saturated with product. This is crystal gazing, but give it your best judgment on its potential. You may want to be ready to expand the line, diversify

or produce the next hot item. Demand is a snapshot of the market today. Tomorrow it may change.

DO YOU HAVE BUSINESS SAVVY— MANAGING, SALES, MARKETING?

Good designers don't necessarily make good business-people, but those who succeed in the woodworking business are usually both. To make a product requires all your skill and ability, the proper design sense, craftsmanship, tools and facilities. To bring the product to market requires skill and ability to market and sell yourself and your product, and the proper setting that draws and entices potential clients to a location that is suitable for your product.

Both sides of the business will need your attention—both sides need to be managed. You can read the numbers to know how well you are doing as of a certain point in time. This applies to daily cash flow,

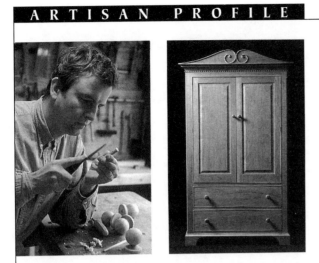

NAME: **Charles Shackleton, d/b/a Charles Shackleton Furniture**

LOCATION: **Bridgewater, Vermont**

PRODUCT: **Handcrafted furniture**

SINCE: **1990**

TRAINING: **Farnham College of Arts, Surrey, England**

SHOP: **18,000 sq. ft. refurbished textile mill**

PRICING: **100 percent wholesale**

AFFILIATIONS: **Simon Pearce, Sawbridge Studios, architects, designers; small showroom at the mill.**

Charles Shackleton Furniture started business in 1990, after a lengthy association as a glassblower with Simon Pearce, who remains the major customer of his handmade furniture line. Shackleton trained, along with his potter wife, at the Farnham College of Arts in Surrey, England. Now employing 30 people using hand tools to shape his furniture, Shackleton grosses $1.3 million each year with his business, which is based in a converted woolen fabric mill in Bridgewater, Vermont.

Q What event launched your change to woodworking?

A You only live once, and I was a young person, and I knew I loved making things out of wood, and I knew that I could run a business and I wanted to try it to see if I could do it.

I always loved woodworking, since I was a kid, and people said "Don't ruin a good hobby," but Iloved making furniture; surely that's what I should be doing in the middle of the day and not on the weekends.

Q What major obstacles have you encountered?

A I think one of the biggest obstacles was lack of self-confidence—particularly with the finances. I think the trickiest side of the business is the money side.

But people are different. Some people can't deal with people to save their lives. For me that is easy. For other people the financial side is easy. It varies. I got more and more confident with the finances when the business had been around longer, but that has been the most gut-wrenching side. But the company has always made money.

Q What are your plans for growth?

A I have no plans for growing the company. I really don't want to manage something too large, but I would like the company to keep developing quality that still has the flavor of handmade furniture. I plan to continue to learn about other furniture, pursue new ideas and fill this 18,000-sq. ft. building with furniture.

We will develop new lines that meet our needs. If someone has an appreciation of what we do, we will be more inclined to work with them, and not just take orders for what someone wants built.

Q How does your niche, Irish Cottage furniture, work into your business?

A It's more sophisticated than Irish Cottage. I don't have a name for it. I've heard people call it "transitional" whatever that means. But it has a feeling of Shaker; it has a feeling of Irish traditional furniture. The reason we have 30 people is not to make tons more furniture, it is more to give us a broader range of skills. Things like wood turning. We now have a full-time woodturner, we make balls, make accessories, we make our own upholstered furniture, and we also are getting more and more into wood carving.

It's really not like a factory in that people are pushing the job along. They work more like cabinetmakers, and they're benefiting from working as a group, whether it is sharing machines or sharing and enjoying working with a group and team to get the job done.

Q How much of your output is going to galleries?

A About 80 percent is through galleries like Sawbridge. We have one very big customer, Simon Pearce, maker of handblown glass. I worked with him for six years, partly because I was looking for someone who was making a handmade product and making a living doing it. Having watched him and learning from him, I decided that I would love to do what I always dreamed of doing, and that is making furniture.

Simon Pearce is about 50 percent of our business, Sawbridge is about 17 percent. Probably a bit more now. We have architects, designers and smaller stores that we sell from, all done on a wholesale basis.

Q Do you do any consigning or commissioned pieces?

A We do commissioned pieces if a customer loves our furniture and wants us to design something that is specifically for them. If they have a feeling for our furniture it could be a new product we might want to experiment with. We try three or four new things a year, either my design or a customer's idea. But we don't custom make things that we're not interested in developing and making more of.

Q When you first started out, did you follow the Simon Pearce format or did you look at gift shows, craft shows?

A When I left Simon Pearce he was horrified, thinking I was going to grow up in his business, and he thought I was crazy turning my hobby into a business. But after I started on my own, he came to see what I was doing. And he has been our major customer from the start.

I did one craft show four years ago, and Paul Zurowski, of Sawbridge Studios, was the only major customer we got out of it. And he actually didn't even come to the show. He called the show organizers who told him, "This guy would be perfect for you." He was looking for woodworkers. Some have come and some have gone with him, but we've stuck it out with him. We are very oriented to selling through stores.

Q How would you rank the importance of quality, design, craftsmanship and pricing?

A Well, this is very basic, but you have to have a product the customer wants. I believe that most of our customers make that decision before they think of any of those other things. What I've noticed, and what I believe to be the way people buy, is they basically walk into a store and say, "I love that piece of furniture." And most of them, if you ask them that instant before they start analyzing, think of it as a work of art; they're immediately taken by it. Initially, I don't think they would be able to tell you why. It is then that they start looking at the details to see whether it all adds up to see whether their original instinct was right. Those four things, the quality, design, craftsmanship and price, are the things the customer then looks at after they have made a decision on whether they want to buy.

Most important, I think the quality and craftsmanship being sort of the same thing is number one. Obviously the design has to be right. It has to do with a certain quality or feeling that you get that makes you feel good, and then I guess that has to do with quality or craftsmanship.

Design I call a technical shape. That is different from a feel or shape. You can have a piece made by two different people, the exact same design, that has a totally different feeling, and just by the way they use a hand plane, or by the way they finish it, there is a certain feel. They interpret it different ways, and that is really what our furniture is about. It has a certain feel to it that people like.

And pricing is important. Our pieces are quite expensive so people are not buying because of the price. Hopefully customers, having that good feeling about it and having looked at the craftsmanship and design, will then accept the price. But I think primarily, the customer has to want that piece of furniture.

My goal is not to have the world own a piece of our furniture. I don't want to manage a company that has to provide that. But it is more to have people aspire to having our furniture. Just like you might aspire to having something in a museum, you know you can never have it but you like it and you think that would be a lovely thing to have in your home. As long as people are aspiring to our furniture, you will always get one or two who will be buying.

Q **What is your legal form of business?**

A An S corporation since about two years ago, and-dbefore that as a sole proprietor. We got into borrowing money, it gives you some legal protection.

Q **What has been your year-to-year sales growth?**

A On the average of 20 percent a year. Our sales this year were $1.3 million, and last year they were just over a million.

Q **How many full-time employees?**

A We have 30 employees—most are furniture makers; 3 upholsterers; a woodturner; an accessory maker producing trays, mirrors, boxes; a business manager; a workshop manager; and a bookkeeper. And we have a small workshop store.

Q **When you started were you self-financed?**

A I took out a home equity loan, a mixture of a straight loan and line of credit. Then the next was an SBA (Small Business Administration) loan for the building. The bank did do most of the work.

Q **Did you find the requirements outlandish?**

A Not at all. We borrowed a portion from the Vermont Economic Development Authority, which was a low interest loan at about 5 percent. They loaned about 40 percent of the project after we occupied the mill building.

the overall performance and the return on your invested time and money. This is a dynamic exercise that changes daily, and can shift rapidly and drastically as your business matures.

Starting out you will probably have to do it all. A good designer and artisan may not be the best marketer, salesperson or manager, but your desire to start a second business is a good indication that you can do all these things yourself until your business grows. Then you can look into delegating some responsibilities or hooking up with associates to share these supporting tasks.

CREATING LUCK—HOW TO BE AT THE RIGHT PLACE AT THE RIGHT TIME

Associating with the right people, being an active member of a business-building organization, talking with others at shows or even out in public places can lead to contacts or suggest a need you can fill. Keep your eyes and ears open to opportunities.

Mingle among other producers and buyers. Build your Rolodex with a list of sources and talents. A referral today may mean a reciprocal commission tomorrow, or "selling" yourself and your specialty may fit a future need of someone you can help today.

You can be your own publicist, having a resume or catalog handy when an opportunity arises. Become a news source for upcoming newsworthy events. Maybe issue an occasional flyer or press release on what it is you're doing; offer to do the same for associations you affiliate with.

"What I recommend when people taking my classes ask how to get started is to go home and get your neighbor, your sister-in-law, or somebody to call the local newspaper and say, 'I've just stumbled on to the most incredible thing. There's a guy over here on Elm Street who's making chairs from logs. He gets these logs, he splits them up and is making these incredibly beautiful chairs. I just thought you guys ought to know about it.' "
—Michael Dunbar (see profile in chapter seven)

By listening to the wants and needs of retailers and even prospective clients, you will be better prepared to target a market that will fill a specific need. Go on a niche hunt.

IN THE FINAL ANALYSIS

"How Much Can I Make?" is the beginning chapter because all else hinges on this critical question. You can continue to produce fine woodwork as a hobbyist, artisan or whatever title you prefer and stay completely satisfied and rewarded for what you do.

Who is making money in woodworking?

Those who excel at design/craftsmanship *and* have good business sense have a leg up on the venture—a flair for marketing, a feel for where their best market lies in product, market and locale.

People-oriented people are often natural market-ers. Disciplined people can force themselves to do it all, even though there is no love lost, understanding that each facet is a critical path toward a successful venture. Finding your niche market and designing/producing a product that fits that niche is key to believing in yourself and in what to promote and sell—at a sustaining profit.

Will the business drive you?

Perception changes when the diversion becomes the driving force. In the following chapter, we deal more with this question of, Can you work for yourself? which is expanded to include, Can you still enjoy creating if the objective shifts from wants to needs, to either supplement or become your sole source of income? This is a weighty question, and as important as, How much can I make?

Do your interests also include running a business? We talk about tackling other aspects of the business; being able to do the other things necessary to manage—to administrate, to keep the books, to marketing and sales promotion, sales and collections. Will you become enslaved in the effort, or are you disciplined enough to get it all done and still have time with your family and for yourself.

Obviously the demand of time and resources during certain phases of the business must be met by commitment, then your attention is focused on the next need, but on balance, can you get it all done and still enjoy it? If the answer to these and other questions that you raise is "yes," go on to test your skills and interests to see if the rest of the chapter topics are for you.

If business is not for you, it is equally rewarding to stay where you are and enjoy your hobby. 'Tis far more prudent and wise to recognize a failing or shortcoming (or interest directed elsewhere) prior to committing funds and effort into a venture that does not have 150 percent of your attention and effort.

Or, you can quit your day job and get on with it.

2

WHERE DO I BEGIN?

Look at the reason you are considering building an income from woodworking. Define why this appeals to you, and look ahead at whether a business would enhance or undo the enjoyment you find in woodworking.

You may have already begun. You are already one step ahead of many start-up ventures. When starting fresh, you have the skills, but perhaps not the tools or the shop you need to ply your trade. If expanding an existing interest or hobby, you are probably already equipped with a cache of woodworking skills and tools acquired over time. And, if coming from the business world, you have also acquired business skills that can be combined with your woodworking resources. The experience you gained from your employment world adds to the skills and knowledge you apply to your woodworking venture.

This is as good a time as any to ask yourself:

- What do you like to make?
- Would you still enjoy making it:
  as commissioned pieces?
  under scheduling deadlines?
  in a production mode?
- Are you self-motivated?
- Can you survive start-up?
- Can you make the money you desire?

DEFINING YOUR PRODUCT

Find a need and fill it. These are easy words to parrot, but one of the most challenging tasks that stand between you and your success. This is a piece of sound advice for any business venture. Maybe you have already found a need and a product, encouraged by results from your early efforts. Or you may be without a specific product idea. Woodturners, carvers and furniture makers have unique skills that can be applied to thousands of design styles and products. Which will work for you?

The fact that you are considering building an income from what you make indicates some level of success and a promising potential from your effort. Encouragement may have come from a request for something to be built (commissioned work), or strong sales results from a local craft or art show, or a favorable acceptance through a gallery.

Ask yourself what prompted these interests. Was it craftsmanship, design, product? Is its appeal temporary? There is nothing wrong with bandwagon hopping, but be prepared to offer something more lasting or more timely to catch the next wave of consumer preference. Be ready to rethink and move on.

Is your product salable at your price? Earlier prototypes received accolades from friends and family, but will the public pony up? You can find out by doing your own market research, without spending $5000 on a study.

Become a sponge. Gather as much information as you can. Ask around—peers, retailers, gallery operators. People in the galleries and shows know what is selling based on the sales niche they have defined and the items they showcase.

Subscribe to design and woodworking magazines, design annuals and show catalogs, or borrow them from your local library. Review these, not to copy, but

NAME: **Bob Stevenson**

LOCATION: **Chula Vista, California**

PRODUCT: **Antique restorations, furniture, Windsor chairs**

SINCE: **1987**

TRAINING: **Self-taught. Brushed up at Palomar College.**

SHOP: **800 sq.ft. building/work area in back of residence**

PRICING: **Commissioned work and consignments to galleries**

AFFILIATIONS: **Word of mouth, referrals, local Design in Wood show at local Del Mar summer fair**

After retiring from the Navy, Bob Stevenson built a hobby of furniture restoration and building into a second-income venture. Schooled in the art of making Windsor chairs with Michael Dunbar as his instructor and mentor, he is trekking cross-country to log his materials for his own line of Windsor chairs.

I caught up with Bob as he was preparing for a cross-country trek to cut some maple and oak logs in New Hampshire to go with the pine seats he has ready for a new batch of Windsor chairs.

Q What event launched your career in woodworking?

A Probably the moment of decision to either stay in medicine after retirement—I was a physician assistant in the Navy—or do something I like.

Q Who or what was most helpful?

A Most helpful probably was the woodworking program I took at Palomar College where I learned some new approaches and changed some old bad habits I'd picked up along the way.

Q What was the most valuable skill you brought to the business?

A Probably my like for furniture finishing and my overall craftsmanship skills.

Q What major obstacles have you encountered?

A The same as my first answer—my decision to give up a more secure, and maybe more lucrative, career in medicine for something I enjoyed doing.

Q What are your plans for growth?

A I have been developing new finishes that are a bit more environmentally friendly to continue my antique refinishing. I enjoy that work, but it could be abandoned in favor of my new interest—producing Windsor chairs.

Q How did you get started in your current venture?

A I did a few commissioned furniture pieces and did a lot of restoration work. That began by establishing a relationship with a local furniture retailer—doing restoration work on commercial furniture damaged in shipping from the manufacturer.

Most of my referrals are for restoration work. I have established a couple of clients who are collectors. One collects Nakashima furniture, so I do a lot of restoration work for him. I have studied Nakashima, so I know the different finishes used in the Nakashima shop in Pennsylvania. The finish is a rather unique one that he [Nakashima] kept secret for years, and it is still a secret, but by talking to people who worked for him and visiting his shop, I have basically been able to figure out the recipe so I can reproduce it on the collector's pieces.

Another collector has a 17th-century bed I'm getting ready to modify into a queen-size. He is not as interested in maintaining its originality as he is being able to use it, but then again retaining as much originality as possible. That's the way I have established my client base, by doing a real good job, and being very conscientious about the work. Clients don't hesitate to refer me to somebody else.

Q You mentioned environmentally friendly finishes. What problems are they posing for today's woodworker?

A With the EPA (Environmental Protection Agency) and OSHA (Occupational Safety and Health Administration) restricting the chemicals used to strip and to renew the old finishes, that end of the business will be more difficult to keep up. The new products don't cut good finishes. I could go across the border to Arizona where environmental laws are not as strict, although we share the same air, but that opens up problems I don't need.

Q What galleries are you in?

A A few galleries have picked my work. I do what I call a "Naka-knockoff," a Nakashima-styled desk. One is in the del Mano gallery in Pasadena; and I have a Federal Period card table in MPLA, a Solano Beach gallery. The card table is priced too high, but it generates referrals for other work.

Q Where do you get most of your work?

A The way things worked out, I keep busy through referral work, gallery interest and the annual Design in Wood show.

As a member of the San Diego Fine Woodworkers Association, I have recently taken over as superintendent of the Design in Wood show, which is an exhibition of woodcraft that runs in conjunction with the Del Mar Fair. I have tried to redirect its content away from craft into more fine furniture and woodcraft.

Q How would you rank the importance of quality, design, craftsmanship and price?

A Quality is utmost in importance. Craftsmanship is a close second, or even hand-in-hand with quality. In design, I try to contribute my experience and expertise, even in reproductions of traditional design.

Q Do you strive for a base labor rate?

A I target for $25 to $30 an hour for shop time. If it is field work—going elsewhere for furniture restoration—it is $75 per hour because I have to bring much of my shop to the site. I always forget something, so there is a good deal of travel time involved.

Q What has been your rate of growth?

A As a retiree from the Navy, I got along just breaking even for the first three to four years. After getting an established clientele and a good referral network, sales have increased 10 to 15 percent a year. I prefer to stay a one-man show. My wife helps with the bookkeeping.

Q What's in your future?

A I may drop back on some of the restoration work and devote more time to the Windsor chairs. I have studied Michael Dunbar, who is an expert on the subject. I took one of his five-day classes and videotaped it for students at Palomar College.

to get a sense of what is being done, what is big and where your competition lurks.

Size up your competition

Wander through a street fair or art show to see what products are being shown. Visit some high-end galleries and take note of the type and price of work they showcase. A juried show, that is one that accepts work judged by a panel of experts in the crafts, can be an indication of what types of designs and products are receiving accolades and ribbons. Look, too, at what isn't there. Answers to questions such as, What is missing, and why? can be revealing when setting your sights on a niche market.

Enter a show or exhibition with what you have, or build a piece specifically for a critique by a set of judges or a target market of buyers. You may not win the blue ribbon, but you will gain some insight of the public perception and a more universal level of appreciation for your work.

It might be helpful to join a local and national woodworking/craftsperson's association and become an insider in the producing group. Not only do you get inspired by what others may be doing, but you'll glean some insight on the direction the business of woodworking is headed.

Avoid a market saturated with third-world products. You can't compete with the low price levels, where your material costs alone sometimes are as much as the finished product, including the retail markup. Your version of a widely available product may command premium pricing, but can it be made so premium as to sell at a profit? It is best to shy away from competitive products already flooding the market where profit comes from low margins on high volumes.

What needs will your product fill?

Consumers are motivated by many things—function, craftsmanship, prestige, nostalgia, price. If you have found acceptance in your test-marketed item, the consumer is obviously motivated to buy. Take a closer look at *why*, and determine whether many more consumers of the same persuasion can be found and enticed to buy. Your product has a style, a look, an appeal. If you can pinpoint this appeal, the sales momentum can be continued through a whole line of products or variations on the design.

Identify the right market for your product, and the best way to reach your customers. Determine which is the best outlet for what you make, at the target price.

If you retail directly to the consumer, consider:
- Festivals—street fairs, annual events, Renaissance fairs
- Craft/art shows and exhibitions, both regional and national
- Commissioned pieces—referrals by designers, architects
- Showcase homes—local redos and seasonal home tours
- Allocating a space in your shop or home for a gallery

If you plan to pursue sales through retailers, look for:
- Galleries that cater to your target clientele—fine woodworking or theme galleries in your style or purpose.
- Gift shows—crafts, gifts, toys, culinary wares. Maybe piggyback with other craftsmen or exhibitors.
- Retailers—specialty stores. Product specialty can be culinary shops, Shaker shops, antiques and replicas, contemporary furnishings or whatever attracts your prospective clients.

Sharing the going price

Woodworkers have a legitimate need to earn a good return from their endeavors. Retailers have like needs as well. If you intend to sell through retail shops, look at both sides to strike a winning balance. Build and nurture symbiotic relationships with shops that will enthusiastically promote and move your work.

How much room for margins on your product will dictate whether you can provide custom items in quantity, at your target profit, and still allow the retailer room to mark up cost to the retail level?

1. Find a match for what you make and what the shop owner sells.

2. Establish a good working relationship and keep a dialogue going.

3. Deliver quality, quantity and on time.

4. Stay alert and open to long-term changes, keeping product in public favor.

If the retailer's required markups will price the item out of reach, and there is no room to negotiate wholesale prices, alternatives might be to consign pieces at a more favorable percentage, look into an artist-run gallery or enter a co-op venture with artisans who make and sell complementing wares.

Theme outlets—specialty shops in style (Stickley, Shaker, Country) or purpose (furniture, kitchenware, garden) or handcraft (fine woodworking, turnings, boxes)—can draw clients to your wares, buffer you from retail interaction (allowing more time to produce) and bring in referral work (maybe at the cost of a referral fee). In a theme environment, a buyer of a Shaker hatbox will see your Shaker chest of drawers (and vice versa). Theme retailers provide a filter by attracting interested, and hopefully more qualified, buyers of your product.

Tom Stockton, profiled in chapter three, has found a good match for his Arts and Crafts and Stickley products through a San Francisco gallery—the Craftsman's Guild. The name has a connotation of both quality and popular styles of furniture and appointments.

DEFINING YOUR BUSINESS AND PERSONAL GOALS

Where are you now, and where do you want to be?

We talked in chapter one about how much you can make. That is only a part of your goals and objectives. Your sights may be set on intangible rewards: spending more time doing what you like, expressing yourself in the items you produce, gaining control of your time and your life.

It might be helpful to rank and rate your goals and objectives into a list of musts and wants. We all want many things, but the musts, although fewer in number, are the key to opening opportunities for the wants.

Taking the time to make a list, like the one shown in the table on page 32, will help you direct your resources toward achieving the critical building blocks for success. Some of the early wants will become musts as success allows.

Each objective also can be ranked with a value of one to ten to give weight to its *impact* on the business. Another ranking is that of *difficulty* or *expense* to achieve, which can shed light on where, when and at what level your attention and resources should be directed.

When identifying your list of objectives, you usually *get* what you *set*, so if you set objectives that are realistic, yet challenging, you'll have a good chance of getting those results and meeting your objectives. If objectives are set too low, or you don't aspire to progress, your lack of success will probably happen. You have created a stagnant, self-fulfilling prophesy.

BUSINESS QUIZ—DEFINE YOUR STRENGTHS TO START AND OPERATE A SUCCESSFUL BUSINESS

Are you self-motivated?
It helps to have disciplined work habits and an inner drive, to help you to remain motivated when outside pressures tend to draw you away from the task at hand.

Can you set and attain goals?
You should have vision to see where you want to go and recognize the best path to get there. Review those goals frequently to remind yourself of the values that sparked the endeavor.

Do you work well independently?
If you are the type that needs frequent pats on the back and a few "attaboy's," these strokes are earned only after you have paid your dues.

NAME: **Jon Sauer**

LOCATION: **Pacifica, California**

PRODUCT: **Ornamental lathe turnings**

SINCE: **Part-time turning, 1981. Ornamental turning, 1986.**

TRAINING: **Self-taught**

SHOP: **Garage with specialty lathes and engravers**

PRICING: **50 percent wholesale and 50 percent retail**

AFFILIATIONS: **Began with street fairs. Now in galleries and some major national market shows.**

Jon Sauer is a part-time woodworker, full-time supervisor with the postal service. He wholesales and retails intricately patterned turned items made on antique ornamental lathes and a rose engine lathe set in his garage in Pacifica, California.

Jon started showing his wares at street fairs, craft and art shows and galleries. He has a show booth ready to ship and set up in a couple of hours. A vinyl backdrop with flaps closes off the pyramid acrylic showcases, tables and cabinets when the booth is not attended.

From the part-time venture, he does 3 to 4 craft shows a year and shows in 10 to 13 galleries across the country. His work has been featured in numerous publications, including *Fine Woodworking*, *Woodworker West* and *American Craft*. Major exhibitions include Smithsonian Craft Show and Gallery for Applied Art in Munich, Germany.

Q What event launched your woodworking venture?

A The cohabitation in a garage with a lathe. I used to raise tropical fish as a hobby. Those need constant care, and I was looking for something I could do, then walk away from for six months, then come back to it.

Q What obstacles did you encounter?

A Acceptance in what I am doing. In the eyes of the retailer, and maybe even the customer, being part-time doesn't command the same respect a full-time artisan may have. People seem to view you and your prices differently if you also have a full-time job.

Q After retirement, what are your plans for growth?

A I am thinking about opening a gallery, and considering some possible locations, to include works besides my own in different mediums to give buyers a choice.

Q How long have you been selling your work?

A I did my first street fair in about 1979 and did them until 1981. Then I did a show when I sold nothing, and I thought to myself, *Since I sold nothing I had better have another way of selling my work*. So in 1981 I decided to go into galleries and market my work that way.

Q How did you get the word out to galleries?

A What I did was send slides of my work for their review, or walk into a local gallery with samples and a portfolio. From 1981 to 1992 I didn't do a single craft show. I did wholesale only, and word-of-mouth business picked up.

Plus, I would send slides of my work to every woodworker and craft magazine around. Sooner or later if the work is good enough, and they need a picture badly enough, they'll print your work. So by continually pushing my work out that way, the word got out. So having my work published in magazines has given me recognition.

Q How many outlets are you selling through?

A I currently deal with about 11 or 12 galleries. The most I ever did was 26 in one year. I decided that was too much. A dozen is a comfortable number of galleries for me [at the rate he wants to produce]. My work is in about 4 or 5 galleries in California, 1 gallery in Seattle. I have some in New Mexico, Chicago, Milwaukee, and a couple in the southern states that I just took on, and in Massachusetts. So that is the spread of my involvement.

Q How do you find these galleries; what is your approach?

A Right now, the way I pick up a new gallery is to do a wholesale craft show, where retailers buy crafts and art. They look over your work and decide whether they want to purchase it. It depends on whether they have the clientele and location to sell my work. They know what they can move.

Q Is this through the ACC shows?

A Yes, the American Craft Council [ACC] shows. I've done the San Francisco one for many years, and I have done the Baltimore one, which is the big one back east. And I do the Roy Helms show in San Francisco and Santa Monica. He has a wholesale catalog and I have picked up some gallery interest from there.

And there's also word of mouth. A couple years ago I had a gallery in Germany contact me, and I followed up on it and did a show over there. It took a bit of time to get my money out of there, but I did very well—I sold a few thousand dollars worth of merchandise.

Q Have you done anything large or only ornamental turning?

A Prior to 1981 I made a lot of different things, but in 1981 I streamlined and just went exclusively into turnings. Subsequently, in 1986 I switched over to ornamental turnings with the purchase of an ornamental turning lathe, for which I had been looking for some time. That avenue of ornamental turning is different, and I have to educate people how I make these things.

I'm also teaching. I've given numerous talks, including one at the AAW at Davis California this year. This past year I spoke at Kansas City. I have given talks at Stanford University, educating people on how I make things, and also why I make things. I make things for two reasons: first, for the pleasure, and second, I'm in it for the money.

Q What is your current proportion of wholesale to consignment to commissioned pieces?

A Commissioned pieces are about 5 percent, consignment 45 percent and about 50 percent are bought from me outright. When I say outright I mean orders, automatic orders, and also retail. I have shown at six retail shows in the first eight months of this year, and that's it for me this year. I need a break from the traveling and running around, so I'm taking a seven-month break from shows until next spring.

Meanwhile, I'm producing on a smaller scale, and I'll be both wholesaling and consigning it. Christmas is coming and I have enough orders to keep me busy. I keep the price the same for what I sell at retail and what the galleries charge, so the price is the same to protect the people who have already purchased my work.

Q How do you determine what goes to direct retail and what the galleries get?

A A gallery in Taos sells everything I can send them. They called just before a show, and I told them they would have to wait until after Labor Day weekend. I needed what I had for a show and didn't want to part with pieces I could sell at retail and make more money. As it turns out I didn't sell as much as I had anticipated. The grass always looks greener, but then sometimes it isn't. But, if I don't sell it one place, it will sell someplace else.

Q You have enough galleries lined up now, but are there a number of new galleries you look at each year?

A When I did the ACC show in August, on Wholesale Days you put up a poster with your wholesale and retail prices, and whether you will accept new orders, or if you will accept names for a waiting list. I indicated I wasn't looking for new sources—I have enough customers. If you're doing this part-time, you don't want to take on too much.

One year I was in 26 galleries and I almost died. This year Neiman-Marcus approached me. If Neiman-Marcus placed an order I'd be dead. I would either have to get additional help or quit my regular job, and my regular job is working for the postal service. I have pretty good benefits and 29 years in, so I'm going to stay until retirement. I can't afford to quit the postal service, even though the wood-working is lucrative, and I can make good

money doing this, I don't want to give up the other. I would much rather get a paycheck every month and know I don't have to go out in the shop and work. That can wait until after retirement.

Q You're pretty much presenting your product as you want to produce it. Do you listen to shop owners as to what they might need?

A I listen, but I only throw in about 10 percent of what people suggest. And the reason is that I'm not dependent on what people tell me because I have a main salary, so I'm in a position to make what I want to make and what I think will sell.

Most of the time I enjoy the work, but sometimes not, especially just before a show when I want to finish pieces and I am in a hurry and trying to get so much done. So those are the times I don't like it.

Q So you're looking at craft shows and galleries as two separate entities?

A Yes, but I don't want to ruin the relationship with the wholesalers, because the wholesale customer is the only way I survived for a dozen or so years. I don't want to totally cut them out. The people who gave me my chance, my opportunity, I'm still giving them work on consignment. And still try to do my retail and not step on their feet. They're in business too, and without them I wouldn't be where I am today.

Q How would you rank the importance of quality, design, craftsmanship and pricing?

A I have to have quality, and quality and price go together. If I don't have quality, I have to throw it away. The customer will know if I'm trying to offer them garbage. I turn out quality work, not quantity, and I get a halfway decent price for my stuff, although I've been told I'm too low. The average person can't afford my work—I couldn't purchase my work. My work is for the people who do purchase my work. When they write me a check, it usually says M.D. next to the name. That is the level that I've moved up to. I'm pleased with the level it's at, and where I am. My stuff sells.

Design? My design is good. I would like to improve on my design. I have lots of ideas, but no time to execute them. I would like to work on a chess set, and that is 32 pieces that might take me six months to do it. Maybe when I retire.

Q What is your legal form of business?

A Operating as a sole proprietor—chief cook and bottle washer. My wife, Sharon, contributes to the work. She does some of the finishing. But when you're a woodturner selling signature work, you're the only one producing, but there are other jobs that Sharon does, like keeping up the mailing list, and on the computer keeping track of everything.

Q Without divulging how much you make, what do you consider your year-to-year increase in income?

A Business growth? A slow start, sending out resumes and photos to galleries and magazines. Business has leveled off to the volume I can handle between the two jobs—playing post office and the woodworking venture. The second income from woodworking represents 40 percent of our combined income.

It's at a level I'm comfortable with. I don't want to go any higher because of the "tax man." The more you make, the more you have to pay out, although I could write off more by doing different things—shows and traveling and all that. I've raised my lifestyle with the business, which is pretty good.

Q How many hours a week do you think you have to put in in order to get this 40 percent?

A I like to work for two hours at a crack. The reason is my hands get sore after two hours (with tendinitis), so I want to do two hours a night. Except I usually will not work on Mondays. So I work two hours Tuesday through Friday, after the kids go to bed. That's the only time I work, and maybe a little on Saturdays and Sundays. But figure 10 to 15 hours a week is what I'm doing, and that's about the max.

When getting ready for a show, I will work probably 25 hours, and that's the two weeks prior to a show, and that's a lot. But that is so I have all my ducks in place. I want to go into a show with a good selection, and it's usually too good a selection and people can't choose.

Do you believe in your product?

You are your best marketer, and your unyielding belief that what you produce is better than your competitors' goods and is priced reasonably for value to the consumer (and reward for yourself) can get you through some uncomfortable criticism, which most often comes from selling to the wrong market sector.

Do you believe in yourself?

Any doubt about yourself might portend disaster, especially when one or more setbacks are encountered. Keep the faith in yourself and in what you are doing.

Do you believe in your pricing structure?

Justify your prices however and wherever you set the value on your time. Be ready, not to defend but to remind the clients of the value they are buying. There are positive motivators whether you are selling wholesale or retail.

Are you a people person?

Reading people and communicating effectively promotes business relationships between the craftsman and his clients. Be ready to talk and to listen, and to help the clients find and feel good about their purchases.

	MUSTS	WANTS
Start-up Phase:	Design and produce a quality, salable product (line)	Break into major markets
	Realize an adequate return on invested time and money	Take early retirement within _____ years
	Break even in year _____	Add help by year _____
Operation Phase:	Buy a _____ to double the output	Relocate operation to _____ by _____
	Build wood storage racks	Buy or build new workshop/ gallery by _____
Marketing:	Get into a national show this spring	Hire a marketing representative to double sales

Ranking Your Musts and Wants

Would you still enjoy woodworking as a business?

It is one thing to tinker in the workshop and another to produce with the same care, feeling and enthusiasm when making one or multiple products for sale. The pressures of quality design and craftsmanship and scheduled delivery can be wearing. It is always more satisfying to make something at a comfortable pace for someone you know will appreciate your work.

Can you accept criticism?

There are ways to avoid direct criticism, which is the desire of many of the artisans profiled here, but it isn't always avoidable. Even the most successful, well-entrenched professional woodworker can be affected by an offhand remark or unpleasant encounter. Reflect on your strengths and consider the source. But also listen and perhaps learn from the input.

Do you have one or more exceptionally strong abilities?

A good design sense is critical, craftsmanship is mandatory, but these traits go unheralded if the business is not managed and promoted with equal ability.

CAN YOU WORK FOR YOURSELF?

Answering no to a few of the previous questions doesn't mean you won't excel. Listing your weaknesses will focus your attention on getting better prepared or finding other means to get certain things done. No single answer will ensure success or bring about failure, but when considered together, a look at the full scope of your outlook will be your shopping list of things to do in preparation for success.

The main question is: Can you work for yourself? You may be considering leaving your vocation for your woodworking avocation for a number of reasons. If one of those is to regain control over your work life, ask yourself whether this lack of control was self-induced—that is, will you find yourself consumed by your new venture, just as you were in the one you left behind?

Team players may find it difficult to solo. They may miss the needed comradery and support from employer and fellow employees. An office party for one won't work for them.

"Attaboys" will no longer come from your superiors, but from a much smaller support group of clients and co-craftspeople (if any attaboys at all) and maybe from good working relationships with suppliers and retailers in the form of referrals, decorator studios and architects you work with. Although much satisfaction comes from being judged on what you produce.

Being focused means always looking for new ways, new markets, new prospects. A social encounter can become a marketing opportunity. Continue to learn, expand, experience business things. Search out new ideas for designs, processes, markets.

Being goal oriented lets you set and get; that is, set

reasonable, challenging goals and achieve them systematically through the old 90/10 rule of success—that is 90 percent perspiration and 10 percent inspiration.

Being disciplined, put another way, involves doing things that don't particularly interest you. It doesn't matter how you accomplish these mundane tasks—eagerly, graciously, reluctantly or begrudgingly—they still need to get done.

You can do what you like to do. But can you do what you don't like to do? Can you divide your time between essential business tasks with equal fervor, care and focus? Some of the business-related activities you will encounter include:

- creativity
- craftsmanship
- accounting
- marketing
- sales
- collections
- publicity
- research
- scheduling
- purchasing

Another well-known number combination used in business is the 80/20 rule; that is accomplishing 80 percent of the task in the last 20 percent of the time allotted. This may work when dealing with a single task, but with ten tasks, such as those listed above, the 20 percent of the time is shared by ten tasks, leaving only 2 percent of the time to accomplish each. Not only must you *do* these tasks, you must be capable of switching gears from the creative to the mundane and back without affecting the mind-set or the results.

MANAGING YOUR TIME

On balance, your time will be distributed between producing, selling and managing. Over any given year, your time may have been distributed as shown in figure 2-1 (page 34). The amount of time you have allocated to the mix will fall into a pattern. As your business matures, your personal involvement in each discipline may change with added help, but the re-

sources will be spread in a similar pattern.

Throughout any given year, demands on your time will be stretched toward the critical tasks of the moment, as shown in figure 2-2 (page 35). You may spend 100 percent of your time for long periods getting product ready for a show, then the demand will shift to dedicating a weekend or longer manning that show, followed by a day at the computer catching up on your paperwork. If the time spans for any of these activities is too prolonged in any one direction, don't ignore the supporting activities that keep your business on track.

Can you make enough to cover your cost of living?

- **Household expenses.** Get a handle on these expenses, if not already known.
- **Shop expenses.** Hold these to a reasonable level relative to the expected return. Look at used pieces of equipment, which are often built better than today's offerings.
- **Insurance.** Continue what you have, and expect insurance costs to go up to cover the business. Review your life insurance coverage. You probably bought to replace income in the event of your untimely demise. As the business grows, the coverage should grow with it. Disability insurance may not be available if working from a home-based office/shop. If your business is separate (or just separated from home) coverage might be available.
- **Worker's compensation.** This is for employees only, not for the self-employed business owner.
- **Health insurance.** Group insurance may not be available, but it is not the panacea it once was. Individual policies are expensive—you could be looking at $10,000 per year. However, you have more options on plans and deductibility that represents what you need, rather than what you gave up with the day job.

A working spouse can bring home the bacon and the health insurance for yourself and your family. Michael Dunbar has taken advantage of today's tax laws by employing his spouse in the business expressly for the advantage of writing off the full cost of employer-provided family health

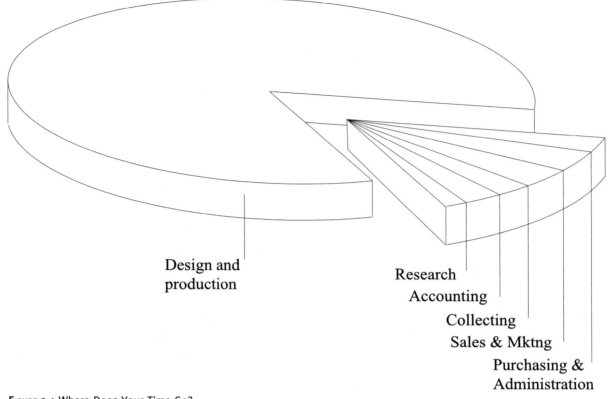

Design and
production

Research
Accounting
Collecting
Sales & Mktng
Purchasing &
Administration

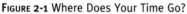

FIGURE 2-1 Where Does Your Time Go?

insurance for her family (himself). Tax laws change, but today about 30 percent of the self-employed's health insurance is allowed as a write-off. Recent legislation has proposed an increasing scale to reach 100 percent in a few years.

- **Property/casualty insurance.** Homeowner's insurance may not cover home-housed equipment used in the business, such as your tools, your shop area, your computer. Vehicle insurance may fall under this same ruling if you use your vehicle for business purposes.
- **Liability insurance.** An umbrella policy might cover you in our litigious society. Consult your insurance agents (life and health, and property and casualty) for specific answers and direction. After substantial growth and expansion, you may want to investigate getting some product liability coverage.

DEFINING YOUR FINANCIAL NEEDS

In chapter one you set some objectives with respect to what you expect from your woodworking income.

These probably resulted from a blue-sky, assume-the-best exercise. Here, you need to look at costs. Not only the cost of materials and equipment needed to produce the product, but your own financial obligations that must be met by the financial return your business will provide.

Can you self-finance the start-up, or will you require outside backing? The Small Business Administration (SBA) bowed out of the lending business years ago. But selected commercial lenders provide small business loans and lines of credit under SBA guidelines. The SBA does maintain a fund to guarantee loans covering the lender should the borrower default, which is only about 2 percent nationally. This low default rate is due in part to the extensive screening and qualifying process.

Special financial considerations for older woodworkers

Young Turks were known for their ambition and drive. Older "Turks" may have those same qualities with less time to exercise them. Whatever part of the finan-

Consider where you apply the time devoted to your business (100% of full or part-time). How will you distribute that time between tasks?

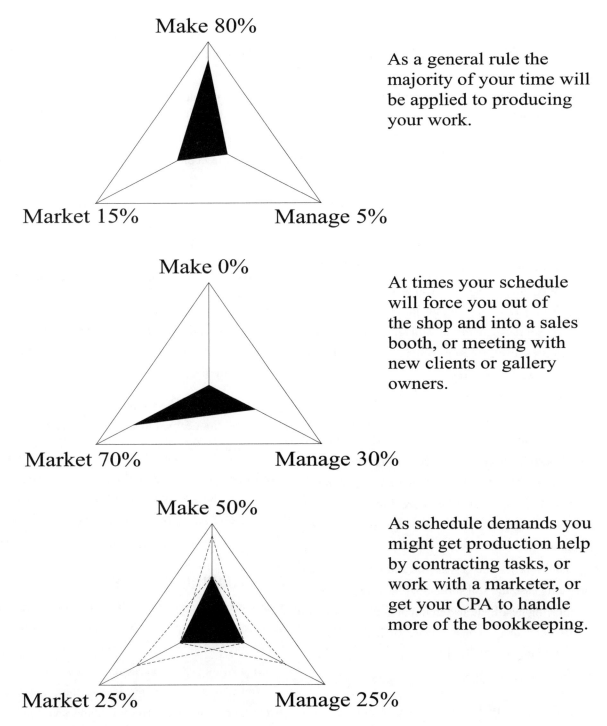

As a general rule the majority of your time will be applied to producing your work.

At times your schedule will force you out of the shop and into a sales booth, or meeting with new clients or gallery owners.

As schedule demands you might get production help by contracting tasks, or work with a marketer, or get your CPA to handle more of the bookkeeping.

FIGURE 2-2 Stretching Your Time

cial resources committed to any endeavor had better net a respectable return without unduly risking the whole wad. Those in the younger crowd can start on their second million (after having given up on the first); they have time on their side.

Nobody enters a business with a plan to fail, but circumstances that could stagnate or shrink a business may be beyond control. Health surprises, accidents or economic conditions could jeopardize your invested capital. Liability, either real or frivolous, can quickly drain the resources.

If considering using your retirement funds as seed money, look at what return on the investment you could get elsewhere, and compare it with the risk/reward of your planned venture. Investing heavily with no real, tested assurance of a return on that investment is not prudent.

Money may be secondary to your business objectives. You may be looking for income to cover only costs of materials, and maybe supplement the pension. Even at this level, your investment should be in line with the intended returns.

Your supplemental income might affect your Social Security benefits, either by reducing payout or changing the percentage of benefits that are taxed based on other income you receive. You may be on the threshold of retirement, where health insurance is not yet available through Medicare. Individual health care policies are at a premium for upper age groups, so budget this into your cost of doing business. There are some tax advantages for the self-employed, but they only ease the still substantial hunk of money.

Staying healthy is also an important objective, regardless of your age. Chapter five contains some things you might do to make your shop a safer, cleaner, more trouble-free environment.

KEEP FEEDING THE RETIREMENT ACCOUNT
Current laws allow withdrawal of your retirement funds, without penalty, at age 59½. The only penalty is the taxation itself, finally shelling out the tax on this previously untaxed money that was sheltered by a Keogh, an individual retirement arrangement (IRA), simplified employee pension (SEP), 401(k), 403(b) or other qualified retirement plans.

You can continue to contribute to these accounts, even in retirement. A portion of your earned income from your business can be sheltered through an IRA ($2,000) assuming your business nets that level of earned income. More can be set aside through a SEP or Keogh plan. Your accountant can direct you in these matters, and your broker or bank can set up the investment activity.

With the economy moving from industrial employment to self-employment, the government is moving toward addressing this change through proposed tax legislation offering incentives for the self-employed, including:

1. Expanding IRA limits for wage earners and their spouses

2. Offering a pilot program for a self-insuring account, tax sheltered funds set aside and available for medical care

3. Amount of health care premiums that can be deducted from earned income is now on an increasing scale

4. A new self-employed retirement plan to replace the existing SAR-SEP, the SIMPLE plan, an acronym for Savings Incentive Matched Plan for Employers to cover the self-employed sole proprietor

FLUCTUATING INCOME
Your income stream will fluctuate just by the nature of your business, especially if your product is seasonal. It may be a while before you can fill the pipeline to realize anything close to a steady income stream.

You may sell pieces outright at the retail price, or outright at the wholesale level; and you'll receive payment on delivery. Other pieces may be accepted on consignment where a remittance will come only after the sale. Commissioned pieces can be, by agreement, full price on delivery, a percentage down (earnest money and funds for materials) or incremental progress payments based on percent completion.

Payment for commissioned or consigned pieces can be delayed if the retailer sells on layaway or on terms. Any such agreement with the retail client should be covered in your agreement with a gallery, or at a minimum, the requirement to get your authorization for such a transaction.

Cash management, discussed in chapter six, provides some tips on cash flow and flow cycle to enhance the return. If after investigating some of the preliminary issues, you are satisfied that a woodworking business is for you, you can now get into the specifics of your operation.

DEVELOPING A BUSINESS PLAN

Setting goals in an informal business plan will help guide your energies toward realizing your ambitions. A business plan will lay out the road map to success. A self-guiding business plan can be as simple as a list of your objectives and a schedule for achieving them.

Preliminary planning

When drafting a plan for your new venture or new direction from part- to full-time, commit to paper any ideas bouncing around in your head. This is planning paper—for your eyes only. Later in your time frame and in this book (chapter eight) you can expand and formalize your ideas, which is a necessary step in seeking financial support, enticing backers/partners, or just staying the course as your business matures.

But for now, jot down the plan. The journalist's approach might help you to structure your thoughts.

WHAT are your objectives, your mission and the product(s) that will get you there?

WHEN will you have everything in place to launch the effort? You're beginning now with this plan, but look ahead to the critical timing—product announcement (maybe targeted for the holiday market), lead time required to make ready, duration of the start-up span for the seed money available, projected break-even point on both the production chart and cal-

endar, and when to expand to the next planned phase.

WHERE will you produce the product? Where will you market the product? Study what appeal your product has and which avenue will most quickly and successfully take you to prospective buyers.

WHY do you want to operate a part- or full-time business? Why will people buy your product? Why is your product superior to the competition's? Why is this endeavor better than other investments (of time and money) of equal or better return?

HOW can you finance the start-up or expansion? How can you produce efficiently? How can you market effectively? How can you build a clientele? How can you bring this all together? How can you grow your business?

Many of the "hows" are topics in this book, but as your business develops, there will be many more that need addressing. Even though the specific needs may not be known at start-up, have some plan to answer them yourself, or through other persons or services you may require.

WOODWORKING IN CYBERSPACE

Anything you've ever wanted to know about everything is probably somewhere in cyberspace, or what we know as the Internet.

Commercialization of the Internet arrived with the World Wide Web, which is evolving into an interactive home shopping network, with text and video and TV and sound, etc., known as hypermedia.

There is a distinction between the Net and the Web, in that a posting of anything that smacks of sales or marketing or self-promotion on the Net is a serious affront to the seasoned users, and the offender can be ostracized or blown from cyberspace for such an attempt.

The Web, on the other hand, is blatant promotion, either as a free site (funded by grants or advertisers) or paid sites where subscribers or users are charged for access to these sites.

Cyberspace can be helpful in planning and running a business, even a woodworking business. A word of caution: New users may be stigmatized by their Internet addresses (@aol, @prodigy, @compuserve) and the accompanying suffix (.com for commercial, .gov for government, .edu for education, .org for organization). Also not being totally familiar with the jargon, syntax and style of Net messages, the neophyte is immediately branded. But don't be intimidated. You're not alone so jump in whenever you have a need.

Benefits of being or becoming a part of that vast sea of information is just that; it is a sea of information available to the user. Hopping on the Net, if you are so inclined and equipped, can bring to you:

1. A broader sphere of contacts through the bulletin boards where noncommercial questions, problems, observations and directions are discussed. E-mail over the Net is quick, easy and more readily read in real time than mail and even faxed messages.

2. Valuable research is readily available on the Net.
   - Starting your own business
   - Business Plan Builders
   - Running your own business
   - Where to show your work
   - Marketing research
   - Product history
   - Accounting packages
   - Catalogs
   - Book dealers

3. Your home page on the Web
   - Building your own Website
   - Linking with other sites
   - Communicating with clients, retailers, design studios, architects

4. Package tracking
   - UPS—http://www.ups.com
   - Federal Express—http://www.fedex.com/track_it.html

5. Getaways/diversions
   - ParkNet—http://www.nps.gov

- The Why Files—http://whyfiles.news.wisc.edu
- Library of Congress—http://loc.gov

Specific online addresses that may be helpful:

SMALL BUSINESS ADMINISTRATION:

SBA home page—http://www.sbaonline.sba.gov

SBA Gopher—gopher://gopher.sbaonline.sba.gov/

SBA File Transfer protocol—ftp://ftp.sbaonline.sba.gov/

SBA online Bulletin Board—Telnet sbaonline.sba.gov

SBA Electronic BBs (computer/modem required):
(800) 697-4636 (Limited Access)
(900) 463-4636 (Unlimited Access)
(202) 401-9600 (Washington, DC, Metropolitan Area)

BUSINESS SOFTWARE:

Quicken, QuickBooks (Intuit)—http://www.intuit.com/quicken; Intuit's toll-free number—(800) 624-8742

Microsoft (full complement)—http://www.microsoft.com; Microsoft's toll-free number—(800) 426-9400

Peachtree (accounting)—http://www.peach.com; Peachtree's toll-free number—(800) 228-0068

Simply Accounting (Computer Associates)—http://www.cai.com; Accupac (also from Computer Associates, Inc.) is their intermediate accounting software package.

BizPlan Builder (Jian)—http://www.jianusa.com; Jian's toll-free number—(800) 559-5426

Direct Marketing—http://www.telport.com/~web/dmginc.html

Amazon Book Store—http://amazon.com

BEGIN WITH THE URL ADDRESS (UNIVERSAL RESOURCE LOCATOR)

http://	www	.home page	.category/	specific page	html

Command to connect to the WWW
 Could also be:
   gopher://
     which brings
     up the WWW
     search engine
   telnet (without
   the ://) to
   link up to a
   teletype BB
	World Wide Web (hyper-media network of graphics, sound, video) file trans-fer protocol (ftp) - is used to down-load files	*Web page or site of sponsor of the information*	.com— commercial
			 .edu—education
			 .gov—
			   government
			 .org—
			   organization
				links to home pages, to spe-cific addresses for the information you seek	*hypertext* mark-up language*

NOTE: Documents in websites are linked by a common word for use by search engines.

And, after you have invested your business profits, you can see how they are doing:

- Securities and Exchange Commission Documents—http://www.sec.gov/edgarhp.htm (EDGAR is Electronic Data Gathering, Analysis and Retrieval system)
- Corporate Profiles— Hoover's Master List Plus—http://www.hovers.com; or Hoover's Earnings Central Page—http://www.hovers.com/earnings/earnings.html
- Stock Quotes (free) from: Data Broadcasting Corp—http://www.dbc.com PC Quotes (up to five quotes per visit)—http://www.pcquote.com Stockmaster (quotes and historical charts on price and volume)—http://www.stockmaster.com Dow Jones Market page—http://djin.com

Get on the Internet via a subscriber's service such as Prodigy, CompuServe or America Online, or access the Internet through services provided by NETCOM, AT&T Worldnet or MCI Internet. Many of these services come with Microsoft's Internet Explorer browser for Windows 95, and being tested for Windows 3.1 and Macintosh. Hundreds of local providers such as CTS Net are also available.

For the novice, some parts of the addresses may seem strange. See the above chart for help in understanding them.

Building your own website is a possibility and is discussed in chapter eight.

3

How Do I Start a Woodworking Business?

Starting a business involves more than hanging out a shingle and opening the doors. What are the issues specific to starting your own business? Here are some basics to help you get started.

If your goal is to supplement your income through woodworking, you can still plan future expansion, or at the very least keep it in mind. By considering future options during start-up you will set the stage for growth, if growth is in your future. *How you begin ultimately determines what you become*—a tag line in a recent insurance company ad that shows a walnut becoming a Chippendale chair—will likely be true for your venture.

BUILD ON WHAT YOU HAVE

Your decision to enter woodworking as a business most likely has some history, some gathered resources, some plan for the approach you intend to take. Your decision to start a formal business may be an outgrowth of something you've done on a smaller scale as a hobby, and no doubt you already have a workshop that got you into this mess. Build on these resources as you lay out your start-up schedule.

Define as completely as possible your start-up needs:

- Product—design, craftsmanship, materials, tools and time
- Facility—space at home, shared space, leased space
- Market—research where and how to market, target markets, indications of interest
- Administration Finances—financing (self- or out-

side), codes and regulations, business licenses, office equipment, business structure, insurance (business and relook at personal), accounting
- Marketing—prospects, portfolio, catalog, mailers, client base

The product

Study the product and the producer (yourself). Do you possess enough knowledge and skill to produce a salable, profitable item? Do you have the all-important sense of design and the skills to transform all of these into a quality piece of value?

We grow with experience. We learn from doing. But you might also benefit from formal study, especially if it will accelerate success. Most of us began woodworking as a hobby or out of a need to produce something for ourselves or for others. We may have bungled and butchered many a project before we hit upon the right way, the better way to ply our craft.

There are lessons to be learned from all woodworkers—those profiled in this book and others—but a close look at how two artisans approached the *business* of woodworking is seen in the case studies of Tom Stockton and Carol Reed, presented in this chapter.

"I knew I couldn't do what I wanted if self-taught, so I attended the woodworking program at The College of the Redwoods in Fort Bragg, and the Primrose Center in Montana, then a three-month apprenticeship with a furniture maker."—Tom Stockton

Many foresaw the benefits of formal training

NAME: **Tom Stockton**

LOCATION: **Petaluma, California**

PRODUCT: **Craftsman style furniture**

SINCE: **1987**

TRAINING: **College of the Redwoods, Fort Bragg, California; Primrose Center, Montana; and apprenticeship**

SHOP: **Shares a converted chicken coop with two other craftsmen: Andrew Jacobson and Mike Flannagan**

PRICING: **Wholesale, commissioned referrals**

AFFILIATIONS: **Sonoma County Woodworkers, California Contemporary Crafts Association (formerly the Bolinas Crafts Guild)**

Tom Stockton, of the three Petaluma purveyors, started his ww business with a decision he couldn't do what he wanted to accomplish if he stayed self-taught, so he got some formal schooling and apprenticed.

Q **What event launched your change to woodworking?**

A Probably when I was 17. I came out to California with my family to visit friends, and I spent the summer in their workshop making outdoor furniture. I continued working for them after high school.

Q **Who or what was most helpful?**

A Lots of different people nudged me at the right time. And I think formal training was essential. I knew I couldn't do what I wanted if self-taught, so I attended the woodworking program at The College of the Redwoods in Fort Bragg, and the Primrose Center in Montana, then a three-month apprenticeship with a furniture maker.

Q **What was the most valuable skill or attribute you brought to the business?**

A Hard work—being willing to do many different things in order to have the time and resources to make what I wanted. And you never know if the person that calls and wants some little thing might want a dining set someday.

Q **What obstacles did you encounter in the beginning?**

A I probably lost a few jobs because of a lack of perceived experience. I knew I could do the job, but the prospect would say, "What? This is your first job?" Also learning how to operate my business. I knew how to build, but it was my computer that helped me organize my business.

Q **What are your plans for growing your business?**

A I'm targeting more furniture jobs and fewer fill-in jobs. Now my time is split, probably one-third of my time doing jobs that keep the work flow going, but these could bring in future furniture work.

Q **How do you go about selling your work?**

A A lot of it is word of mouth, some of it is sales through galleries, and some are outright orders from galleries. I don't get a lot of sales through galleries, but I get orders.

I show in Highlight Gallery in Mendocino and

the Craftsman's Guild—which features Craftsman style pieces—in San Francisco. I'm probably going to be showing in another gallery in Half Moon Bay.

Q Do you have different things in each gallery?

A I get quite a few referrals from Sausalito where I go meet with a client and discuss a custom project. The Gallery in San Francisco—I have done a few Stickley pieces for them—tends to be more orders of my pieces they have on the floor, or reproductions of original pieces, or variations—do this but make it a different size.

Q Are these orders through the gallery or direct retail sales?

A Through the gallery. I don't do any Stickley on spec. It is too competitive a market.

Q Are you wholesaling to the galleries?

A A lot of it is consignment. Some galleries don't buy outright. My consignment prices are the same for everybody. I leave the markup up to them. Some galleries have different clientele and they can charge a higher markup.

Q What percentage do you generally get from a consignment?

A Fifty to 55 percent.

Q And on commissioned pieces through a gallery, would you give them a kicker?

A They get a referral fee that varies but averages from 20 to 35 percent. Sometimes I don't even know. I'll do a referral job and send all the paperwork to them. They mark it up and send their invoice to the client.

Q How many new outlets do you consider each year?

A Not very many. I keep pretty busy. It's a lot of work just to come up with new spec pieces and service existing galleries. However, I approached the gallery in Half Moon Bay on the recommendation of someone else. And the gallery in Sausalito may be closing, so I need to replace that outlet.

Q You are into pretty high-end stuff. When you started out did you look at gift shows, craft shows as an outlet?

A I have never done that. I've tried to get into the ACC Fair and always got wait-listed like number 30 or 40, and it's not really worth it. I think my photos were too much of a hodgepodge of things.

Q Can you estimate a percentage of sales from galleries?

A I would say about 30 percent comes from gallery floor and referral work, and the remainder is either word of mouth or repeat customers. I do some work through designers. They see my work in the galleries, or their clients know of me and we get in touch that way, or another designer recommends me. There are all sorts of ways.

Q Has there been any work coming from publicity?

A None from the article in *Woodwork* magazine. A local paper did an article on the gallery in Sausalito; nothing ever came from that. But I was in the local paper and I got a table job out of that. They contacted me through the California Contemporary Crafts Association, which used to be the Bolinas Crafts Guild. I never expect articles to bring in any work, but they're great publicity and they get your name out there. You can also show them to people and it adds a lot of legitimacy.

Q Do you have any walk-in business?

A We have an ad in the Yellow Pages, but it is mostly, "Can you fix my screen door?" It's not pulling what we are looking for. But I don't turn down any jobs. I had a kid come in here who had cut part of the rocker his dad was restoring to use as a handle for his paint-ball gun. His dad had him in here to "find someone to fix it and you pay for it."

Q How would you rank the importance of quality, design, craftsmanship, delivery and pricing?

A Quality, design and craftsmanship are all on the same level. Design is very important as is quality. Quality and craftsmanship are kind of the same. And I'm pretty good about delivery. I am very rarely late because I tend not to have firm deadlines to give myself a cushion. About pricing, I have been raising prices the last couple of years, so a part of me feels that pricing is important. Even though people may spend money on high-end furniture, they still want value.

Q Without divulging how much you are making, what has been your year-to-year income growth?

A It's hard to say. For the last couple of years it has been pretty steady, and this year I have probably done about 30 percent more in sales. I'm getting more jobs, and some of it comes from getting more realistic prices for my furniture. Bigger jobs have a lot to do with it. I've done about 20 chairs. One job was a set of 8 Greene and Greene chairs based on the Blacker House (San Marino/Pasadena, California, area) arm chairs, and another set was more contemporary.

Q And during the start-up years?

A I starved.

Q Did you see a linear progression of income, or did it finally hit?

A When I started I did a lot of subcontract work. The outdoor furniture place where I used to work would give me almost all the work I needed, making high-end hand-carved redwood furniture. I would do that for a week and make my furniture for a week. I was also paying $85 a month rent on a shop—really low overhead.

Q And the furniture you were making then was on spec?

A For the first couple years all I did was spec work. When I sold those pieces I would make more.

Q During your first nine years have you been self-financed?

A I've never gone out for a loan, except from my parents and they don't count. At times, instead of loaning me money they would buy my furniture.

Q Did you have a marketing approach when you started?

A I didn't have any marketing approach besides knowing that I needed to get into as many shows as I could and knowing I needed to get into galleries.

through woodworking schools and apprenticeships to more quickly and assuredly prepare them to bring their vision to reality—and to market. But that is not a prerequisite to success. To extract a few facts from the Woodworking in America survey (see chapter four), 64 percent of both professionals and amateurs are self-taught, but professionals, as a group, received more training through woodworking schools and apprenticeships.

Even those of us who are long in the tooth and more skilled (we think) in the ways of wood, and design, and art and fabrication, continue to expand our base of knowledge and skill by doing, but we should also consider the benefits of active involvement in woodworking groups, taking advantage of symposia available in almost every woodworking discipline, and maybe even availing ourselves in woodworking curriculum available through local community colleges or private schools.

Any skill and expertise you bring to the business can give you an edge. This could be business experience from past employment or college, a marketing background, accounting, public relations, people skills, combined with your design and woodworking skills prepares you for all the aspects for building an income. Special skills and interest applied to the product can be both the reason for the business and for its success. We tend to do well in subjects we know, bring credibility to what we do, and, as discussed within chapter four, know your stuff.

If you direct your resources toward a specific niche market, which may not be defined at the outset, you can build on both your special interests and expertise.

The tools

A schooled woodworker, after finishing studies and an intern program, enters the business well trained and ready to meet the challenge with her knowledge, but little else. Acquiring tools at the outset is a major part of the start-up costs. And, depending on what she produces and in what quantities, and how quickly she can recapture the costs, this expense can be significant.

But when a hobbyist goes professional, the handcrafted goods may not require a major tool-up. However, look at alternate ways to produce your product more efficiently, which might justify the cost of a gang saw, or a thickness planer, or a multi-router. It is later that you may need to grow beyond what you can or want to self-finance, or what can be financed by the requirements and price of a commissioned job, such as bigger, faster, meaner equipment, or larger quarters.

Even beyond that, your dreams may involve entering an offshoot business venture of opening and operating a gallery, going more into mail-order sales, or whatever else is promising, reasonable, achievable and of interest to you.

Outside financing includes a look at SBA financing requirements for a business loan. By the time you're ready for that phase, you will have established credibility and accumulated the history in the way of financial results for a few preceding years (see chapter

six). You will also have a clearer idea of how much money you will need, for what purpose and the anticipated return that both you and your bank can expect from a bank-funded investment.

The surprises

The more detail you can put in your start-up plan, the fewer hidden costs you will confront. Know what fees are required, what equipment is critical (and what can be purchased later), and what insurance coverage (and its cost) is needed.

Not-so-hidden costs are start-up license fees, estimated tax remittance (both personal and business as a self-employed woodworker), business taxes and insurance. Other unknown expenses, such as repairs when equipment breaks down, will always be lurking. So plug a fudge factor into your estimated costs.

Your sales projections may be based on retailing directly to the end user, but some contingency should be in your plan if you find that working through fee-based shows or wholesaling your goods to galleries better meets your objectives. These estimates will become more accurate with history and experience. Your marketing plan and product might not yet be in sync—out of balance—as was shown in figure 1-2.

ORGANIZATION—LEGAL FORM OF BUSINESS

Starting out, and even staying part-time, requires some thought about your legal form of business, which will most likely be a sole proprietor of a business, whether it is a self-employed venture or a part-time diversion from your regular employment or retirement.

Sole proprietor (self-employed)

A one-owner shop is the simplest, most efficient form of business.

A sole proprietor using independent contractors or part- or full-time employees expands his responsibilities of record keeping as an employer. When adding people to your business, their classification is important to you, and to the government's fair employment

NAME: **Carol Reed**

LOCATION: **Ramona, California**

PRODUCT: **Church furnishings**

SINCE: **1987**

TRAINING: **Palomar College**

SHOP: **Separate shop with storage annex**

PRICING: **Retail—commissioned church and secular furniture**

AFFILIATIONS: **San Diego Fine Woodworkers Association. Teaches in the Palomar College woodworking program. Conducts seminars on routers and router bases. Consults on church furnishings.**

Carol provides a product and service to a niche market segment. She uses her affiliation, knowledge, product, value and project management options to benefit the client congregation. They have a resource and an ally in woodworker Carol Reed.

Q What event launched your change to full-time woodworking?

A My interest started early, when at seven years old and living on my grandparent's farm, my grandfather sat me down with a piece of pine and a plane and showed me how to make curlicues. The smell and feel of the wood did it.

Many years later the breakup of AT&T also broke up a 15-year career. Their out-placement evaluation pointed to doing something with my hands and with people. I coupled that with my love for wood and woodworking into building, teaching and writing.

Q Who or what was most helpful?

A The people at Palomar College. Chris Fedderson and Dave Thomsen have directed and encouraged my efforts. And long-distance mentor, Patrick Spielman through his scroll work books.

Q What are your plans for growth?

A I like the mix of work I do now and want to work them all in—continue designing and building church furniture, taking on secular commissioned pieces as my schedule allows, teaching woodworking classes at Palomar College and giving seminars and talks around the country.

Q How did you get involved in this church project?

A A little over five years ago I was finishing my woodworking program at Palomar College. My finals project was due about the same time the church was soliciting building pledges. The last thing I had was money, so I offered my talent, and my final class project, and they accepted.

Q Do you search out commissions of this kind?

A Yes, I do. And actually this is the only work I try to market. The secular work that comes to me is strictly word-of-mouth. People say, "I would like to have this piece of furniture, and I can't find what I like." I see my forte not so much as a woodworker, although I think I am good at that, but as a problem solver. I hear a different drummer so I see things a different way. I am a very visual person. I look at things and can recognize there is a hole there, but my mind immediately goes to work filling it. And I've done that all my life. So that makes it easier for me to lay out projects, to be able to visualize and know how things have to come together, and know when things must be done to all come together under a deadline.

Financing for church furnishings is often done as a memorial—in the memory of someone. You have a lot of bosses and you have to tread very lightly, because it is generally highly emotionally charged. You have to understand all of the underlying currents that are going on and honor all of those, in addition to delivering the piece that everybody is happy with.

Q Your clientele is different from someone selling through a gallery, but your clients are still as discerning. Can you rank for me the importance of quality, design, craftsmanship, pricing?

A I try to marry personal philosophy with each customer, in terms of what they are envisioning and in terms of what they are prepared to pay for. Based on what I know about churches, having been involved in churches all my life, church furniture rarely ever gets replaced. Since this is a 50-year investment, I remind the organizers not to nickel-and-dime it, or they will be very unhappy.

In terms of design, construction, joinery, finishes—all the details of woodworking—all products are designed with the idea that you are going to be using this for 50 years.

In terms of that, the choice of wood, finishes, joinery, glues are designed with the idea that the furniture will be in a very unfriendly environment. Most churches, and the majority in more hostile environments than southern California, are only heated and cooled when they are being used on Sunday mornings. So my philosophy, the one that I try to impress on my customers, is that this is not a place to be penny-wise and pound-foolish.

We try to work within a congregation's budget, which is the hardest thing to do because they don't often know. You have to go through an educational process. I don't think that anybody who would like to do this full-time to put beans and hamburger on the table will actually make a go of it. I don't think so. I can't imagine that. You have such an educational process from the time of the first contact to the time the check arrives that you starve to death in the meantime. Fortunately there are other things I like to do and that I can do. I tell my other clients that, "You understand that if a church job comes along, I'm gone." That's my first priority. And that works. I can work my other schedules around that.

Q What other types of commissions are you accepting at this time?

A The most recent nonchurch commission I did was for a member of this congregation. They wanted a wall unit—a combination TV cabinet, hutch, computer desk, etc.—done in the Craftsman style to match the one piece of antique furniture in their home—a Stickley style chair. We talked, and we planned and I presented a design, but the price was an obstacle. I proposed doing one module at a time, but got no response, so I didn't bring up the subject again. Months went by and I finally got a call. They had talked with other craftspeople, but were not comfortable with their approaches. Some told them they didn't want the features they wanted. I completed the unit except for the finishing, which they elected to do. I removed all the hardware and delivered the pieces for their finishing. Then, when ready, I went back and we reassembled the whole thing.

Q It seems that you really work with the needs of the clients. What do you charge for your time?

A I try to keep current on my costs. I have a good history of hours and expenses, and I apply these to new jobs, updating the costs of supplies and materials, and I add my labor, overhead and profit margin. I think my last job was estimated at about $33 per hour. For the type of work I do and the time involved on-site, I don't feel I can charge much more than that.

practices, Internal Revenue Service (IRS) regulations and the like.

So when added labor is needed for seasonal or big job overload consider:

- *Subcontracting* the work to a separate business entity, or using a cottage industry.
- Being the master craftsman for an *apprenticeship* program with a local trade school or government work program can be a productive and worthwhile endeavor.
- Bringing in an *independent contractor*, also considered a separate entity—but watch how long and how frequently these people are used before the government considers them employees.
- *Part-time* employees who work for more than half of regular full-time hours in any given week or year are considered full-time. Stay under 20 hours a week and under 1000 hours per year.
- *Full-time* employees on your payroll will open the full complement of regulations by which you must abide.

NOTE: How you classify these employees will determine the labor laws that govern them. *Exempt*, that is, creative or supervisory employees, can be considered salaried employees, exempt from certain labor laws, such as payment for overtime, whereas *nonexempt*, or hourly workers, must be paid at least minimum wage for each hour worked and be paid for overtime. And later on, other employee benefits you may offer at your discretion—sick leave, paid vacation, health insurance, profit sharing—will be subject to regulation in how they are shared and distributed. At this time your company policies must be formalized. Employer responsibilities also apply to employers that are more complex legal forms of business.

Partnership

In any partnership with financial backers or another producing artisan, a partnership agreement is essential. A strong friendship can be torpedoed over money issues. Intent and perspective change under the siege of operating a business, so have legal papers drawn up (from a resource book or preferably an attorney) to stay the course. Partners may all be coproducers, one business/one marketing, or maybe a managing partner/limited partner arrangement. A partnership has some drawbacks other than the mix of friends and money. A partnership is considered dissolved in the event of the untimely departure of one of the partners.

Limited partnership

A limited partnership can be set up to give the general partner (or partners) managing control, but with it comes full liability of the partnership's obligations beyond the general partner's investment, whereas the liability of limited partners is limited to only the amount of money invested, whether these are cash backers or employees on a profit-sharing/incentive plan.

C corporation

A C corporation is structured for some tax advantages and limited liability. A corporation operates as a legal entity, separate and distinct from its owners, with owner liability limited to the amount each has invested. Personal assets are protected under the corporation. However, the owners of solely owned or closely held corporations, especially if newly formed, are often required to co-sign, as individuals, any legal document, personally guaranteeing and making both entities legally and financially responsible for corporate commitments. Here there is no limited liability since personal assets can be attacked and attached to satisfy corporate debt.

S corporation

An S corporation is set up more like a partnership. But unlike a partnership, it is its own entity offering some protection of personal assets, and would continue in the event of the loss of one of the principals, just like the big guys (C corporations). S corporations are not taxed on their earnings. The profits and losses flow through the corporation untaxed, and the taxes are borne by the owners (shareholders) of the S corporation.

If and when you are ready for one of the more complex legal forms of business, your accountant or attorney will be able to advise you based on your business success, growth and your plans for the future.

WHAT'S IN A NAME?

Using your legal given name to identify your woodworking business has some distinct advantages. Some of those advantages are:

- Direct association, linking the craftsperson to the product.
- Market recognition of you and your product.
- No fictitious name filing and public notice.
- No "d/b/a" (doing business as) designation or periodic publishing of fictitious name notices.
- No federal tax identification number (yet), other than your Social Security number, if you use your name. When and if you become an employer, you will apply for an employer identification number (EIN) and will receive by return mail, Publication 15 circular E, "Employers Tax Guide," and some of the forms you must file.

It is the craftsman who should be synonymous with the quality of the distinctive designs produced. Something is lost in the translation when a signature series is signed "The Acme Co."

The state in which you are licensed may require a filing of a fictitious name notice for your part-time business, which is not an insurmountable obstacle. Just remember when applying for business licenses or loans, or entering into contracts, the formal filings for the fictitious business name should be in place.

But your business name is not as important as are your efforts directed toward product and marketing, maybe with some minor thought applied to building an image. But your business image on some early printed material will help you market.

When you, or maybe a graphic artist friend, are designing your business identity (name or logotype), consider the different ways your name or the name of your business will be presented.

Your sales kit might include:

- Biography and photo—states who you are and your credentials.
- Portfolio—photos, awards, newspaper/magazine articles.
- Business cards—with or without a product photo. Hand them out liberally, or have them handy for pickup at shows and fairs.
- Quotation forms—ready for your next commissioned piece for a client or for consignment to a gallery owner.
- Show signage—identity draw to your booth or table, and attractive product placards.

Also consider a hallmark for your product with a name or logo or as a signature series.

Catalogs, mailers, contract agreements for marketing, and the more operational forms such as imprinted checks, purchase orders, invoices need not be customized during start-up, but when you do want to spiff up your image and get your business organized, your preliminary design package can be applied to all your business forms.

You can present an effective graphic representation of your name by spelling it out in a fitting typestyle. Play around with your initials as a graphic element (but not a formal business name), or use your surname, nickname or portions thereof.

Some of the forms you might consider using are presented later in this chapter.

LOOKING AT TAXING ISSUES

Is this a hobby or a part-time business? The IRS will be looking for hobby activity, so the test for a part-time business—profit in one of the past three years—must be met. Good business records give you an advantage and may be your best protection against or during an IRS audit.

If you operate as a sole proprietor, the IRS will require you to classify your endeavor when you file Schedule C, Profit or Loss From Business (or Schedule C-EZ, Net Profit From Business), with your Form 1040 each tax year. Instructions to the complete 1040 tax filing package contain the activity codes to use on your return, which will most likely be 0836 for Lumber and other wood products, 0810 for Furniture and fixtures, 6883 for Authors and artists, or 8888 for Unable to classify.

Other tax forms you or your tax preparer will be using include:

- *Schedule SE* to pay self-employment tax on income from your trade or business.
- *Form 4562* to claim depreciation or amortization of assets or to report information on listed property. You can also choose to expense (write off a portion against earned income) a part of the cost of certain property you bought for use in your business, also contained with Form 4562.
- *Form 4797* to report sales or exchanges of trade or business property.
- *Form 8824* to report like-kind exchanges.
- *Form 8829* to claim expenses for business use of your home.

Consult IRS Pub. 334, Tax Guide for Small Business, for more information.

Instead of heading to your local IRS office, taking a number and standing in line forever, you might be able to get the information you need on the Internet. You can do this a number of ways:

telnet to "fedworld.gov"

file transfer through "ftp.fedworld.gov"

check the Web at "http://www.ustreas.gov"

LICENSES AND PERMITS

The federal government will get theirs. Plus most states, counties and cities have their own bureaucratic menus of regulations. A long list of requirements shouldn't scare you away from your plans, but as your business grows, the more complex and regulated things will become. For starters, and especially for part-time supplemental income producers, only a few of the following requirements are required initially.

Local members of trade associations or independent operators of similar small businesses can give you some direction in what's needed in your locale.

SBA's Small Business Resource Guide lists such things as:

- IRS Federal EIN (sole proprietors can use Social Security number) from Employment Development Department
- Federal Requirements for Employers
- State Worker Compensation Regulations
- State Board of Equalization for seller's resale/sales tax permit
- City Business License/Business Tax Permit
- Zoning Use Permit/Home Occupation Permit for home-based business
- Property Tax and Personal Property Tax for business equipment and furnishings
- Fictitious name filing if name other than the owner's
- Occupational Safety and Health Administration (OSHA) issues
- Environmental Health Permit
- Air Pollution Control Permit
- Fire Code Inspection (for home-based businesses)

Remember that this is a list of regulations from a larger city. County and rural areas still find ways to generate tax revenue, but requirements may not be as long or as stringent as the examples shown above.

Oasis Press publishes the series *Starting and Operating a Business in . . .* , by Michael D. Jenkins. It has a version for each of the 50 states and Washington, DC. Your library may have a copy, or thumb through it at the bookstore to determine if it is something you could benefit from.

WHERE TO GET HELP

For new businesses in general, the SBA has scads of leaflets, programs, help groups and a library of helpful information for the start-up company. They also assist with ongoing company concerns. Their SCORE program provides one-on-one consultations in many disciplines related to running a successful business, and the SBA holds local and national seminars and meetings, some in conjunction with other organizations that can be most helpful to your business.

The local Chamber of Commerce, maybe under their Small Business Development Program, offers similar helpful aids geared more toward the ongoing businesses who may need to polish or refine their approaches, or find themselves having to comply with the growing regulations brought about by a growing company.

BEING THE EMPLOYER

Employee may be the feared "*e* word" for many sole proprietors, but a sole proprietor doesn't have to be a sole producer. There may be times when your workload demands jobbing out, or bringing in independent contractors, or hiring part- or full-time employees. As business owner, and therefore potential employer, each level of employee classification opens a different level of requirements. Labor laws, reporting requirements, taxes withheld, reported and remitted, all grow along with your staffing methods.

Having a trade-in-kind arrangement, especially for those who share shop space, can work well. Even craftspeople in the same community who don't necessarily cohabit workshop space can form an alliance that may begin with reciprocal referrals and then, if schedules permit, assist one another in sizeable tasks.

The next informal arrangement might be to job out work to an independent contractor for a specific duration. But any prolonged use of an independent contractor could be construed by the IRS as trying to bypass the labor laws and taxes normally shared by the employer.

Payroll records are critical to you, your employees and the "tax man." Your accountant, if you have one, can guide you in the employee forms you must file, and the IRS conducts a Small Business Tax Workshop nationally, which details the requirements for the small business owner. There is probably one held in your area. These are a few of the forms to file.

• Form W-2—Wages and earnings for each tax year, or portion of a tax year. These include a year-end summary of all taxes paid on behalf of the employee, such as the employer's share of social security and Medicare tax, and those deducted from the employee's salary, remitted to the government and credited to his account.

• Form W-4—Employee specifies number of exemptions to be used in calculating the withholding tax. The employee may also designate a dollar amount for additional withholding.

• FICA—Social Security.

• SDI—State Disability Insurance (non-work-related), which is separate from workmen's compensation that covers *workers* injured on the job.

In a part-time or start-up venture, you may not be concerned with payroll accounting, but with success will come the potential to expand your management operation to address and satisfy all that is required as an employer.

However, you may elect to be the employer of your business partner to take advantage of a full deduction of health insurance premiums for the partner and his or her family, or to increase the family's contribution to a retirement plan. All these approaches are legal and may hold some benefit in your situation. As of this writing, these laws are changing with respect to self-employed health insurance deductions and the limits on self-directed retirement plans. Check with your accountant or financial planner for the latest information on limits and deductibility.

INSURANCE

Workers' Compensation

Workers' compensation insurance is available only to employees of your company. It is also available, and may be prudent to get, to cover on-site contract work, other contractors, independent or employed, working on your facility and with machinery. This is like a home owner's policy covering mishaps while any type of service worker you hire conducts business on your property.

Liability

In this litigious society, a little money spent for added protection may be wise if you believe it might be needed and is not too cost prohibitive. An umbrella policy can override your other insurance. Errors and Omissions insurance really doesn't apply, but other product liability insurance for small toys, utensils, furniture that may not be prudently put to use, are events to consider, but not lose sleep over.

Wooden toys, for example, are made of flammable materials and can also be hazardous in the hands (or mouth) of a small child, who would rather chew than pull your pull toy, or stand on a chair rather than sit in it. Insure if you can, but ensure the product is as foolproof (and there are a lot of fools out there) as possible—splinter-free, nontoxic wood and finish, etc.

Customers visiting your workshop should be kept out of harm's way. A separate area, maybe with a separate entrance, could help prevent a mishap with your power tools or a trip over a clamping jig.

If you sell through galleries, ask if their coverage also covers you in the event of a mishap involving your product that they sell or even show. If a customer's child climbs the open drawers of a tallboy and it topples on him, find out who is liable in the event of a lawsuit.

Business casualty

Working a business from your home may exclude business-related equipment and space from coverage on a standard home owner's policy in the event of a disaster. Check with your indemnity agent to add a rider listing the business portion on your coverage or to write a new policy.

SPECIAL CONSIDERATIONS FOR RETIREES

No matter what reason a retiree wants to operate a business—to keep active and busy, to expand skills, knowledge, associates—the level of success can impact the savings and pension income already earned for your retirement. Income earned in your woodworking business can adversely affect the favorable tax treatment of, and even reduce, your Social Security benefits.

According to the Social Security Administration, even if still working (or earning an income) you may qualify for benefits. Until you reach age 70, there are limits on how much you can earn without losing some or all of your Social Security benefits. These limits change yearly. Upon application for benefits, you are told what these limits are at that time, and if working (or self-employed) income would affect your monthly benefit, and those of your qualified family members. Earning limits also apply to family members who get any kind of benefit on your record.

Use of funds reserved for retirement income should be revisited often. Unless you have a 150 percent assurance of a good and timely return on your investment, don't be tempted to buy a new workshop unless you can be assured that the costs will be returned in a reasonable amount of time, and with a hefty profit margin. Otherwise, go slowly and prudently in your new venture.

More of the everyday operational concerns, such as maintaining your health and safety, comfort and lighting, and other personal and preventive measures, are discussed in chapter five, "How Do I Set Up My Shop For This?"

OFFICE ADMINISTRATION

Some time must be spent on the administrative side of your venture. Whether you do so in the beginning or your spouse or a budding business partner does it, some time has to be devoted to keeping you, and the business, on track.

Whatever skills and interests you bring to the administrative side of the venture is a bonus and further assures your success, whether you personally participate or hire someone you know will do the job.

That task of office management, can encompass various levels of:

1. Bookkeeping

2. Accounts payable

3. Accounts receivable

4. Cash flow

5. Inventory control

6. Buying

7. Contract administration

8. Accounting
   - financial reports (balance sheet, profit and loss statement)
   - net worth
   - tax return preparation (estimated quarterly returns, year-end returns)
   - payroll tax filings
   - sales tax filings

9. Records retention

10. Cost analysis

Other hats you might wear include:
- Public relations/publicity
- Sales and marketing

Or you may step onto the dock and become:
- Shipping and receiving
- Inventory control

Being a computer-literate person will help you conduct your business with a tool to accomplish and control many of these tasks. A PC would be helpful, but not essential. Unless you are somewhat computer savvy, learning computer skills and producing product for your business may be spreading you too thin. But there will come a time that you will see the efficiencies a computer can bring to your business. Some of the applications for which a computer can be useful include:

FINANCE:
- Return on investment, cash flow, accounts receivable
- Future value of money
- Resale status and reporting requirements

- Tax filing status—cash or accrual method
- Write-off of capital equipment—depreciation

RECORD KEEPING:
- Chart of accounts—what should be included?
- Cost of goods sold
- Cost analysis and estimating—what is your time worth?

How you might approach compiling and crunching these numbers is presented in chapter six.

Cost accounting method

You have two choices, and your tax preparer or accountant will guide you in this decision. The *cash method* is where income is recognized when it is received or set aside for your use, offset by amounts actually paid during the tax year for deductible expenses. The *accrual method* requires you report income when you earn it and deduct expenses when you incur them, even if funds are not received or paid during the tax year. Rules are contained in IRS Pub. 538, Accounting Periods and Methods.

"What to ask" is the message here. There are far too many variables specific to your circumstances and locale. Chances are that although some answers will change from place to place, the nature of the question will be of concern and needs to be addressed.

Sometimes a business evolves unintentionally, fed by its own momentum, or through some serendipitous action of being at the right place at the proverbial right time. No conscious effort was expended on the formalities. You just did it! But there should be a time when you look back and ask yourself, Did I do everything right?

Management and administration of your second business

When producing supplemental income, your efforts will be less formal and may not require some of the business forms described below, although some might be helpful.

Much of your work may be on speculation (or "on spec," as they say), and some from word-of-mouth referrals may bring on commissioned work. The source of work will dictate how formal and extensive your billing forms need to be.

- Client forms:

  quotations—make effective for specified duration, spell out what will be produced and within what time frame.

  purchase agreements or contracts—may be prudent if the magnitude of the effort so dictates (incremental payments are to be received, delivery scheduling incentive bonuses are available, etc.). Agreements can dictate delivery (on or before a specified date for a fixed price) and time and materials (a fixed amount or a variable amount not to exceed X dollars.

  invoices—should be all you will need to bill the client (if necessary at all).

  statements—usually a summary of multiple purchases within a billing period. Not a consideration for the part-timer, or even full-time artisan working on spec or commission and watching the cash flow closely.

  remittance logs—list of your sources of income. They tie directly to your bank accounts and are helpful in calculating cash flow.

- Suppliers:

  purchase orders—agreements to buy described items at specified prices, delivery methods and costs and dates.

checks and check ledgers—for a start-up company, can be a universal record. The checks written against the business account can be coded for the chart of accounts you may produce monthly or at year-end.

- General:

  fax cover sheet
  business cards
  placards
  point-of-sale ID
  catalog

Your accountability system could include job numbers or client identifiers that can be linked or keyed to the cost of producing the sold item. This information can link to the accounting method you use, and also to the marketing and sales portion of your business.

Similar to the work flow through your workshop, the flow of information through manual or computerized databases (see chapter six) will help you stay the course in the most effective and efficient manner.

Where to find these forms

Office supply stores and warehouses will have off-the-shelf forms or form sets for the small business owner. PC users can get into the office type utility programs and use the default forms or customize them to meet specific needs. Or you can start from scratch in designing what best suits, and represents, your business.

4

HOW DO I KNOW PEOPLE WILL BUY?

The marketplace is filled with high-tech products that fill our homes and offices. Most consumer products are professionally designed and efficiently manufactured, but they are obviously a product of stamped parts in injection-molded housings. Their lack of individuality is contrasted by products crafted from the trees, from the hands and sometimes from the heart—fine wooden furniture, appointments and accessories produced by today's artisans.

Today's discerning buyers want something unique, something special, something beautiful, either as a gift or for their own enjoyment. So, there is a market out there for what you make if—and that's a big "if"—you make what they want, need and will pay for. A simplistic answer to the question, Will people buy what I make? is *yes*—if you make what they will buy.

> "Well, this is very basic, but you have to have a product the customer wants. I believe that most of our customers make that decision before they think of quality, craftsmanship, design or price."—Charles Shackleton (see profile in chapter one)

TARGET YOUR MARKET

Before you get into the specifics of "How Do I Price and Sell My Work?" (chapter seven), your sights have already locked on a broader, not yet defined, target marketplace, maybe not consciously, but by the nature of what you intend to produce and where you intend to sell. Your sales efforts may be best targeted toward:

- craft shows, street fairs, exhibitions for *direct retail sales* of things you have produced on spec

- galleries and specialty retailers, and maybe even craft shops, contacting owners or operators in person or contacted through regional or national shows to *consign* or *wholesale* what the galleries feel they can move

- commissioned sales *at retail or with a referral fee* can generate from past products or through advertising, networking, word of mouth or direct referrals

Regardless of which market you initially target, client interest and demand may cause you to branch into another marketplace. A commissioned piece could result from showing at a street fair, or a gallery piece may be the source for producing a variation or an altogether different piece of work. Networking through existing clients, and even the woodworking suppliers you frequent, can bring in work, if you take the time to let them know what types of work you do.

KNOW YOUR STUFF

Your creativity is a salable commodity, whether you produce a uniquely designed contemporary product, an authentic style reproduction or a representation interpreting a design style.

In contemporary work, a good sense of design brings all you put into your work together—proportion, shape, material, finish, function, comfort—all the creative sense you apply to what you design and produce. These products stand on their own merit for what you have created, and the visual, tactile and functional pleasures they invite. This applies equally to small accent pieces, accessories and furniture.

Reproducers of furniture styles in past movements and methods echo the creative sense from past designers and artisans. Become a student through study of the products, their producers and the methods used in the original style to create a dimensional replica. Period furniture and accessories, whether in the French Provincial, Queen Anne, Empire, Windsor, Shaker, Arts and Crafts styles, all have a place in today's market. And there is an astute following of period styles as well as styles based on the works of an individual who made his mark in the world of furniture and decor, such as Chippendale, Sheraton, or Stickley. You need to get into their heads, and into the heads of the buyers to know what it is that draws them to the style.

If making interpretative replicas of furniture or accessories, you are operating somewhere in the middle ground, handcrafting reproductions with a sprinkling or large dose of artistic license. Your interpretation of these past styles or eras will determine its appeal to different tastes in the market, depending on how loosely or strictly you follow, or capture the essence of the design in your work. Many clients are knowledgeable in the history of their favorite styles and appreciate the knowledge you bring to your product, especially if it is a commissioned piece.

Other crafts require other expertise with equal study and preparation. If doing bird carvings you need to be an external ornithologist; when building model ships, you must become a shipwright in $\frac{1}{32}$ scale; or if your market is building church furnishings, it helps to become just as knowledgeable in the ecclesiastical ways as you are in the ways of crafting the product.

"My clients are very knowledgeable, because my prices are now high enough that the people are not just buying my model ships on a whim. A lot of them are collectors and historians, and are knowledgeable about the ships. In fact, a lot of my clients furnish the blueprints and history on the ships."—Myron Van Ness

WHAT'S HOT TODAY VERSUS YESTERDAY AND TOMORROW?

Trends change, markets become saturated with the latest craze, and clients move on to other fads, looking for what is in vogue. A survey of the top crafted merchandise was compiled by *Woodshop News* in 1994. Current trends are presented in figure 4-1 (page 59).

Boxes have led the pack (15 percent of the total items mentioned) in recent times. They possess the charm, feel and personality of handcrafted wooden products, yet are more affordable than furniture and obviously sell in greater volume to a larger buyer segment. Occasional tables, kitchen utensils and turnings of all types as a group account for 20 percent of the top twenty listed products.

And this survey doesn't address what styles of these most popular items are in vogue. Client preference may not have changed in the type of product, but certainly has in the style in which they are made. Whether you make these products, or products that complement or contrast them, you should know where the market is headed and your place in that market.

It may not be wise to enter a market that is saturated with products full of mass-producing competition.

BEGIN WITH AN EDGE

According to figure 4-2, there are 18.5 million woodworkers in the U.S. and over 7½ percent (or 1.4 million) consider themselves professional, with more, such as yourself, in the pipeline considering entering the business. What will set your product apart—what is your edge?

You don't need to start from square one. If what you want to make is newly in, or just coming into vogue—that is, following social and demographic trends—you have sales momentum on your side.

Your product can drive the search for a market, or the market can drive your product. Balance your product-to-market, and target the best locations with the highest proportion of high-prospect buyers. You will probably start, and might stay, in your own area if you

NAME: **Myron Van Ness**

LOCATION: **Laguna Beach, California**

PRODUCT: **Ship models**

SINCE: **1975 (serious model building)**

TRAINING: **Self-taught**

SHOP: **Room in home**

PRICING: **Retail**

AFFILIATIONS: **Exhibits annually at the Laguna Festival of the Arts only**

Myron Van Ness is into a niche where his ship model clients are almost as knowledgable as he is in the art of understanding ship design and executing model building. People will buy if you cater to their interests.

Q What event launched your change to full-time woodworking?

A When I retired from work. While still working I would only do this on weekends and still manage to get a couple of pieces a year out, but now I can get as many as five or six pieces a year, depending on the complexity of each piece. Now I guess I could be called full-time. However, it is not the kind of thing you can sit and do every day. I take a couple days away from it, then I come back and am eager to go.

Q Who or what was most helpful?

A I would say other ship model builders and in particular Ed Simms. He exhibited at the Festival for 30 years. He was my biggest inspiration. And there was an elderly man in Leisure World who did exquisite work. He was retired from owning dental labs and you can imagine the dexterity. He did things that I still can't come close to.

Q What was the most valuable skill or attribute you brought to the business?

A I've always done artwork and worked with my hands. All through school I took art classes, wanting to be an oil painter. And I took woodworking shops, learning how to work with tools. And God blessed me with hands that are fairly manipulative and has not taken my eyes away too much yet. Hand-eye coordination is the most valuable asset. However, I still attribute most of the gift to inspiration from other people.

Q What obstacles did you encounter?

A Time. That is the biggest obstacle. I just run out of time. I'll be in the shop for what I think is a few hours and I've spent the whole day. And sometimes I'll look at a day's work and wonder what I've accomplished, but my wife will remind me of how much I accomplished.

Q What are your plans for growth?

A Keep trying to do finer and finer, more detailed, more complex work. Sometimes I wonder whether I should show at all. I really have no plans for expansion. I've had offers to go overseas and teach manufacturers how to build models for mass production, but this is an art form. Every ship is different. I don't want to get into a production mode. I get upset at mass-produced art.

Q What started your interest in model building?

A I have always lived around, on and in water and always loved boats and ships. When I was a child my father always had boats. It evolved from a childhood interest in the sea and anything to do with it. Early on in life, as a child I started building ship models because I liked the looks of them so much, but they were quite crude. My father took us to museums, and the models in maritime museums just fascinated me. It kind of evolved into, "How could I do this?" Other model builders inspired me and I did a lot of reading on the subject. I have read a lot of history, especially maritime history, and just fell more and more in love with ships. I kept building. They started getting better and better, and I learned more and more techniques through other people (the Ship Modelers Association in California). I learned how these fellows did things, acquired more and more books, especially on collections of model ships in museums (such as the Naval Academy in Annapolis, and Britain, and ships at Mystic and Smithsonian).

I would study them. They were so perfect, and such a challenging thing, how to blend this craft with an art form. I do take some artistic liberties with my colors and try to make them look appealing for people and to look good in their homes.

I had a long friendship with the ship model builder Ed Simms, who showed at the Festival. However, he was such a good friend I didn't want to compete with him. In about 1982 he had a stroke, which left him paralyzed on his left side, so the following year, conferring with him I said, "I think I'll submit my work to the Festival of Arts," and I did, and was accepted and have been in the Festival of Arts every year since.

Q Is that the only place you show your work?

A That is the only place. I get enough exposure from there, enough orders. It's all I can do to fill those orders. In fact, last summer's Festival was so successful I am booked for over a year now. It was a love affair, a hobby that turned out to be somewhat lucrative. My work has gotten fine enough where I can demand a pretty nice price for my pieces, and it is really rewarding. The biggest reward is that my clients are pleased with my work.

Q Before you started showing at the Festival, were you selling elsewhere?

A I was selling through art galleries for probably 15 years. When you first start out, you're almost giving them away, mainly for materials. I have been doing this for almost 30 years. I started to get real serious about it in 1975, started doing finer things, and my goal was and is that every one I build is better than the previous one. Otherwise, why do it?

Q Do you consign or wholesale?

A I do strictly commissioned sales, strictly through the Festival. Actually what I prefer is to build what I want to build and then put them down there during the show, and they sell. Some summers you don't get too many commissions, so I am able to do some things on spec, which actually for me is a lot more fun. I am not as pressured and can do things in my mind rather than what somebody else wants.

Q What kind of inventory do you feel comfortable with going into the show?

A I like to have about four. However, we were victims of the Laguna Beach fire a few years ago and I lost all my inventory. As we speak, the one I am building is the only one I have right now. We don't have a model of our own. I haven't caught up. Business got so good we can't build one for ourselves.

Q **How would you rate the importance of quality, design, craftsmanship, delivery and pricing in your models?**

A My clients are very knowledgeable, because my prices are now high enough that the people are not just buying my model ships on a whim. A lot of them are collectors and historians, and are knowledgeable about the ships. In fact, a lot of my clients furnish the blueprints and history on the ships, which actually takes a lot of work out of it for me, which I appreciate. I can just do the building rather than doing the research, which is very time-consuming. Sometimes information is not available.

My clients are mostly private parties. The models will usually all go in a home, and occasionally in an office. Most buyers don't restrict themselves to just one ship. Most people have two or three. They want a fleet because they are interested in different types of vessels.

Q **What is your business structure?**

A Sole proprietor, self-employed. That is the way I list it on my tax returns and business license.

Q **Do you market the show?**

A The show has a client's day. The artists send out invitations to attend a private showing, which is a good thing for all the exhibitors. Maybe a client did business with another artist the prior year, but this year they may be in the mood for something else. So it helps everybody.

I also get referrals from my clients. But these models take so long, you can get overwhelmed. In fact, spare time is appreciated to branch out and explore some other construction in my mind, and I don't have to worry about meeting a date.

It's kind of a dilemma in a way, whether you want to build for yourself or for others. Sometimes I think, *I don't want to do this anymore.* I want to do more exquisite, finer work, in which case a model might take a couple of years to complete rather than three or four months. Just different types of construction, more elaborate models. Some years I hope nobody wants anything, so I can do some of the things I want to do.

And I am in a unique position. I don't need to do this for a livelihood. When I do sell one it's real nice, but it isn't something I have to do. I don't feel pressured that way. The fellow I mentioned who since passed away, that was his sole source of income. If he didn't get orders it was a terrible thing. He used to price his models based on how much rent he owed. It's just not a good way to do it. But my mind is free, and I think it reflects in my work.

Q **What about financing?**

A Self-financed. Just expand as things allow.

offer a product that is in line with what the buyer is likely to buy. Going beyond your backyard, art, craft and gift shows are planned, assembled, located, timed and promoted to seek out the highest prospective clients and showcase the goods that are in vogue, in demand.

You may not start out reinventing the wheel or changing the social tastes of the masses, but consider future direction of public acceptance and work toward filling a need for the next buying wave. Meanwhile, produce what sells today.

DEVELOP A SUCCESSFUL PRODUCT

Your products carry the full burden of your financial plan, the thing that will allow you to meet your objec-

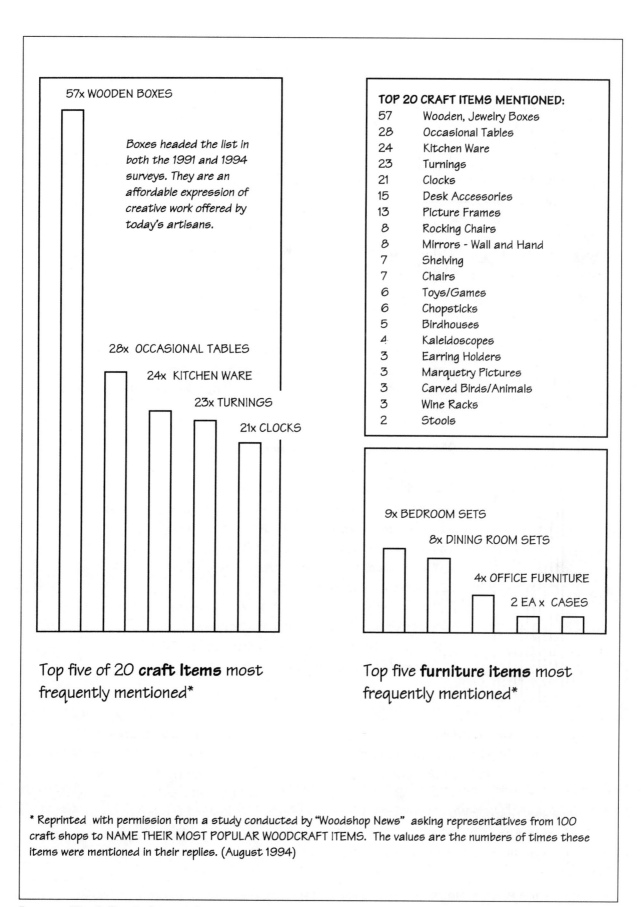

57x WOODEN BOXES

Boxes headed the list in both the 1991 and 1994 surveys. They are an affordable expression of creative work offered by today's artisans.

28x OCCASIONAL TABLES

24x KITCHEN WARE

23x TURNINGS

21x CLOCKS

TOP 20 CRAFT ITEMS MENTIONED:

57	Wooden, Jewelry Boxes
28	Occasional Tables
24	Kitchen Ware
23	Turnings
21	Clocks
15	Desk Accessories
13	Picture Frames
8	Rocking Chairs
8	Mirrors - Wall and Hand
7	Shelving
7	Chairs
6	Toys/Games
6	Chopsticks
5	Birdhouses
4	Kaleidoscopes
3	Earring Holders
3	Marquetry Pictures
3	Carved Birds/Animals
3	Wine Racks
2	Stools

9x BEDROOM SETS

8x DINING ROOM SETS

4x OFFICE FURNITURE

2 EA x CASES

Top five of 20 **craft items** most frequently mentioned*

Top five **furniture items** most frequently mentioned*

* Reprinted with permission from a study conducted by "Woodshop News" asking representatives from 100 craft shops to NAME THEIR MOST POPULAR WOODCRAFT ITEMS. The values are the numbers of times these items were mentioned in their replies. (August 1994)

FIGURE 4-1 "Top Selling Craft Items" from 1991 and 1994 surveys of *Woodshop News*. Reprinted with permission.

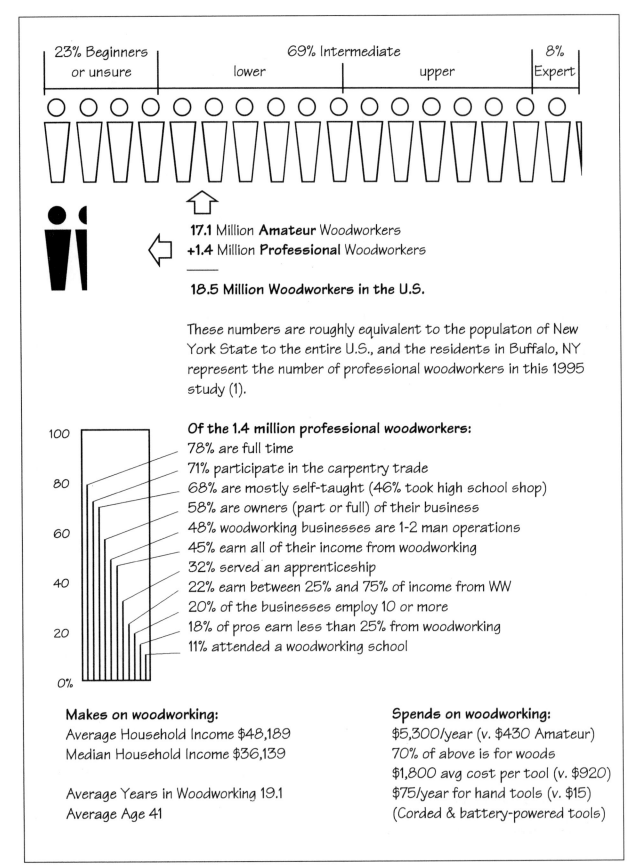

23% Beginners or unsure

69% Intermediate

lower   upper

8% Expert

17.1 Million **Amateur** Woodworkers
+1.4 Million **Professional** Woodworkers
_____
18.5 Million Woodworkers in the U.S.

These numbers are roughly equivalent to the populaton of New York State to the entire U.S., and the residents in Buffalo, NY represent the number of professional woodworkers in this 1995 study (1).

Of the 1.4 million professional woodworkers:
78% are full time
71% participate in the carpentry trade
68% are mostly self-taught (46% took high school shop)
58% are owners (part or full) of their business
48% woodworking businesses are 1-2 man operations
45% earn all of their income from woodworking
32% served an apprenticeship
22% earn between 25% and 75% of income from WW
20% of the businesses employ 10 or more
18% of pros earn less than 25% from woodworking
11% attended a woodworking school

Makes on woodworking:
Average Household Income $48,189
Median Household Income $36,139

Average Years in Woodworking 19.1
Average Age 41

Spends on woodworking:
$5,300/year (v. $430 Amateur)
70% of above is for woods
$1,800 avg cost per tool (v. $920)
$75/year for hand tools (v. $15)
(Corded & battery-powered tools)

FIGURE 4-2 Data from 1995 "Woodworking in America Study" commissioned by *American Woodworker* magazine.

tives—it is the golden key that opens every opportunity. The item you design is not a product until you bring it to market. With that thought in mind, the table on the next page contains a progression that builds toward accomplishing your goals, with each step building on the prior and leading toward the next.

The sequence could change depending on where you enter the list. Some steps can be worked backward, but however approached, early conclusions shouldn't drive the results, that is skewing results to match what you think is so. Be open to input, unbiased in your observations and honest in your conclusions.

Use the scientific method:
- Identify your observation—form a hypothesis.
- Question—pose alternatives.
- Research—find the answers.
- Analyze the result.
- Draw your conclusion.
- Verify.

The ultimate, real-world test is a customer ponying up for your product. Find out if what you want to make will sell, and decide how you will change the product or the target market if it doesn't.

WHERE TO CONDUCT YOUR MARKET RESEARCH

Even before you have a product, you should observe and note what is being done, size up your competition, and get a feel for the marketability of a certain style, line or specific product.

Market research can be as simple as showing your product to a few people in the field and getting their reactions to it. Better still, show it to people in the business—retailers and promoters—and get immediate results, such as on the spot purchases or orders.

CONDUCTING FIELD RESEARCH

A random sampling for mass marketing is an effective way to determine what percentage of the population will be drawn to the store and buy what types of items at what price. Pollsters can get a good idea from a small

random group, how the masses will respond.

Thankfully, you need to know if people will buy only one product or line—*yours*. It is helpful to know what levels of results the gallery or other outlet experiences for their locale and clientele.

When you do field research—visiting galleries and shows—make a mental note of what to record. Or maybe have some file cards prepared as shown on page 67.

TEST THE MARKET

Winegrowers may plant roses around the perimeters of their vineyards, not for color, but as an early warning device to foretell pests that could ruin a season's crop or the vineyard itself. Rosebushes, being susceptible to the same diseases as the grapevines, provide an early warning that the vines are becoming infected. A shorter but more lasting example is the canary lowered into a mine shaft to ensure the presence of air and the absence of poisonous gasses. If the bird comes up alive, the men descend. Victims of technology, canaries have lost their jobs. Testing a product or trying a new outlet can be your rosebush or your canary. If it survives the test, maybe it is OK to go in.

PROMOTE YOURSELF

How many of these sales resources you use will depend largely on how you bring your work to market. If you have the product, the time and the inclination, you can:

1. Self-promote (retail) your work
   - to the end user via word of mouth, publicity or advertising bringing clients into your gallery/ studio. Hold an open house, conduct demonstrations at your shop. Encourage referrals from satisfied customers.
   - to buyers attending shows and exhibitions, including street fairs, local shows, fairs, regional and national shows. These may also invite wholesale, as well as retail, trade to your booth. Be ready with a portfolio, and maybe a start-up kit (as described in chapter three) containing your catalog, price lists and quotation forms.

PRODUCT:	**Need**	Even before a pencil hits paper or the item takes form in your brain, what you produce for profit must fill a need.
	Niche	Once the need is defined, you can narrow your target market, not in the number of buyers or price range, but to tailor your product, or your market or both to balance the two.
	Acceptance	Your tastes, and those of your family and friends may run along the same lines, but might not be timely, or universally shared with a large sector of potential buyers. Test the market. If the results prove less than encouraging, retrace the steps above.
	Design	Now you can create an exceptional design that fills a need and fits the niche of your target market. If your specialty is a specfic style, know that style, whether you are building reproductions or contributing your own design variations to the items.
	Craftsmanship	You must be harder on yourself than the customer might be in expecting and delivering masterful craftsmanship. Value must be both inherent and apparent if you are to entice the buyer to buy at a price that will meet your objectives.
	Quantity	From early analyses, have some idea how many units you need to make and sell in order to meet your objectives, to break even, and begin profiting. Reconfirm that you can produce the quantities required to get the needed results.
	Market	The needs and niche analyses should point to your target market. Find out the locations, and in what numbers these prospects congregate and buy what you produce.
	Marketing	Estimate how many customers you will need, and how many contacts will be necessary to find the desired percentage of buyers. Decide whether the numbers, the price and quantities you're dealing with can be marketed personally, or whether outside marketing in the form of galleries, promoters or sales representatives can better push your product. If the marketing plan works, be prepared to meet demand.
	Pricing	Know your production costs, and the expected level of return on your time and talent. Set a target price factoring in your findings during the acceptance step. Look at, but don't necessarily follow, comparable prices for comparable pieces. Weigh retailers' input and guidance. If this falls short of your expectations, review the above steps and adjust your expectations, product and marketplace.

Selling	Have a good idea of where, and to whom, your product will sell. This should point you to the most effective sales channel, whether you retail it yourself, through local, regional and national shows, or wholesale/consign through galleries or other retail outlets. Wholesalers can be contacted at the shows or directly.
Growth	Gaining success the first time through, or after one or more adjustments to the product or sales approach, or both, will sustain the return from your efforts. Then you can enhance that product or try your next idea following similar developmental guidelines. Build on that experience. Nothing succeeds like success.

2. Co-promote (wholesale) your work
   - through the use of "wholesalers' hours" at the shows, some of which are listed below.
   - through gallery presentations, by mail or walk-in introductions aimed at specific galleries or gallery groups that may be co-ops, associations, local galleries for local artisans or galleries that specialize in the style, mood, function or any classification that may fit what you do.

   The term co-promote is used because you still must market yourself, if not to the ultimate client, then to the wholesaler who will be representing you and your work. To get a gallery owner's attention, or that of a jury board, you need to offer a good product match to their clientele and enthusiastically represent yourself either in person or in the proposal you submit.

3. Prepare bids and proposals
   - If you will be doing one commissioned piece, a set or a roomful of furniture, either following your marketing plan from the outset or as a spin-off from a gallery appearance or earlier work in a client's house, or a featured artisan in a design book, be prepared to "sell" the client on the work.
   - Communication is the key to reeling in the job. You need a lure, hook and net, or it may get away. And that's not a fish story.
   - If the prospective client is interested in a piece identical to, or a variation on, a piece they saw and liked, an exchange of thoughts and a discussion of their needs and wants may be enough to land the job.

   Without the benefit of a past client relationship, a more formal presentation may be in order where neither the producer nor the buyer has a base of reference. Communications might entail the following:
   - Sit down and review your portfolio together.
   - Listen, note and sketch details about what they want, how they intend to use it, where it will be located. Approach the commission just as an architect would when designing a home. Tailor it to the buyer's lifestyle.
   - Communicate an approximate price range. If they are thinking otherwise, it is best to know it early on (again, your rosebush warning device).
   - Ask if a conceptual sketch or drawing based on your understanding of their request would be helpful.
   - Have the commission agreement ready for signature.

Based on the size of the job, and your hunger factor, a fairly formal proposal could help the prospects of making a sale. It need not be grandiose to communicate your care and understanding of the client's needs.

   Your enthusiasm is contagious and will be spread

Photo © Gregg Krogstad, 1995

NAME: **Jennifer Schwarz**

LOCATION: **Port Townsend, Washington**

PRODUCT: **Fine furniture and appointments. Carvings.**

SINCE: **1982**

TRAINING: **Apprenticeship. Oregon School of Arts and Crafts.**

SHOP: **Entire ground floor of two-story residence**

PRICING: **Wholesale, some commissioned work**

AFFILIATIONS: **Member, Northwest Fine Woodworking Association. Shows at the Northwest Gallery of Fine Woodworking in Seattle, The Real Mother Goose gallery in Portland, and major national shows.**

Q What event launched your change to woodworking?

A I graduated from college and needed a job. I started by apprenticing with a finish carpenter in the community whose son—his helper—had run away from home, so I asked for his job and I got it.

Q Who or what was most helpful?

A The man I first apprenticed with was an incredible teacher in finish carpentry and also carving. He gave me my basic skills and paid me $5 per hour. He would teach me something and would be very quick to let me learn by doing.

Q So you had no inkling that you wanted to get into woodworking before that time?

A I've always done art, working mainly in clay, and a lot of things, but I was never exposed to wood. Girls weren't allowed to take shop, and I knew sewing dresses was not my calling in life.

Q What is the most valuable skill or attribute you brought to your business?

A The ability to come up with an idea and keep on going until I get to the finished product that I want, even though along the way it looks like it could never possibly become what I want it to become. And loving to make things, and curiosity. One of the things I like about sculpting is that each time it comes out a little bit differently.

Q What obstacles did you encounter?

A It's really hard to make money at this because the work is so darned slow. The fact that I like doing new and different pieces keeps it slow. And also getting tooled up—it's a huge investment.

Q What are your plans for growth?

A I occasionally get tempted to just design and have other people build. I am not clear about where I want to grow; I know more where I want to go with my work, a more lucrative market rather than more production. The best-paying jobs I've had have been for carvings for institutions and big hospitals, rather than residences, and it's fine, fun work for me. That's a direction I would like to move in.

Q What is your best outlet, as far as sales?

A The Northwest Gallery of Fine Woodworking accounts for 90 percent of my work. I have had shows in art galleries and in other galleries. I really appreciate the screening done by the gallery staff. It saves me a lot of wasted breath. I want the customer to know what they're coming for and be ready to buy at my price.

The days when people would say to me, "I saw something I want, but I want it custom and cheaper," are long gone. I remember that turning point in my career when I said, "You don't come to a custom woodworker for *cheaper*, you come for *special*."

Q In selling through galleries, do you consign or wholesale pieces, and what percent goes to the gallery?

A Strictly consignment. As a member of Northwest Fine Woodworking, my commission split is 30/70, so the gallery gets 30 percent and I get 70 percent. The Joinery Gallery gets only 15 percent, and on second-time purchases it gets only 10 percent. I have an excellent client through them who has come back a few times.

Q Do you seek out new avenues, new outlets?

A I really don't, as long as I have enough work. The last few years have been pretty steady, so I haven't felt the need. I've gotten real spoiled. I used to do quite a few national and regional shows, but seeing how strong Northwest Gallery of Fine Woodworking is, I've gotten real spoiled about just staying local.

Q In the galleries, what is a complementary array of things for your pieces?

A For me, client screening is central, but ambiance is important—some people are expecting to spend thousands of dollars. As far as what my work would go with, I've been in a show that my work was with turnings and photography, which was quite a beautiful complement. I've also been in general craft galleries—Mother Goose—which included pottery, glass, jewelry and other furniture.

Q Describe what you do. How would you classify your custom furniture?

A I incorporate a lot of carving, sculpture in my work, yet there is an elegance to it. So, it's polished out, very refined. These days I'm doing mostly custom work, so when somebody says to me, "I want a desk," usually they're not going to be my client. But when they say, "God, I love your work and I'm looking for a desk. Could you do that for me?" then they'll generally be my client. I'll go to their house, if possible, to see the space and talk to them about what they want, and what they want it to be like, and how they want it to work with the room.

I go for elegance, but I also love doing sculpture, so there's a lot of sculpture incorporated. I recently did a couple of pieces with salmon swimming through a sofa table, a medicine cabinet. Those have gotten an incredible response, so I have many commissions generated off of that.

Q How would you rank the order of importance of quality, design, craftsmanship, delivery and price?

A Quality and design would be first, then craftsmanship. I know I'm not the most meticulous craftsman in the gallery, but I remind myself to look at who I'm comparing myself to. And then pricing; I feel like if I can build it, I can find a market for it.

I meet my deadlines. The only time I don't is if I get sick, because I'm a one-person show, or some radical thing. I'm in constant touch with my clients and they would know about the problem. If I have too much work and a deadline that my client needs, I will sometimes pass a piece on to another furniture maker, a former shop mate I worked with on Whidbey Island.

Go as far as needed to get the job, but ONLY as far as needed. Most times a sketch should suffice.

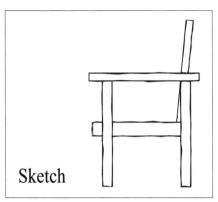

Sketch

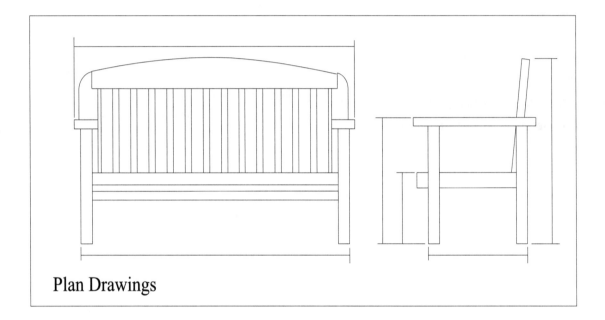

Plan Drawings

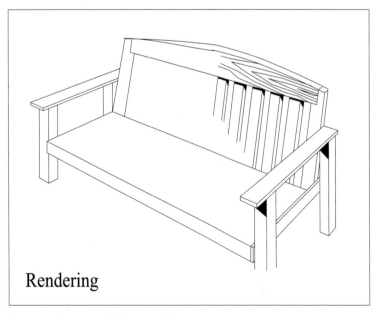

Rendering

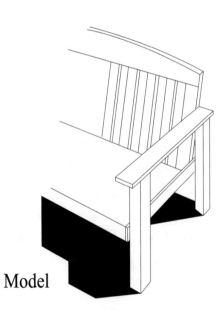

Model

FIGURE 4-3 Conceptual Presentation

```
┌─────────────────────────────────────────────────────────────┐
│  GALLERY NAME:_____    │
│     Address:_____    │
│     Owner/Contact:_____    │
│     Telephone#:_____ Date of visit: _____    │
│     Product specialty or mix:_____    │
│     Price ranges:_____    │
│     Quality of:                                              │
│         Product:_____    │
│         Presentation:_____    │
│         Display area:_____    │
│     Product needs, shortages:_____    │
└─────────────────────────────────────────────────────────────┘
```

Sample research file card

through the gallery representing the product to the ultimate client. Your enthusiasm also shows in how well you craft your item, which creates customer satisfaction, making the gallery owner happy and back knocking on your door. And the process continues full circle again and again. This continuous marketing is important to create and to sustain effective representation and build a symbiotic relationship. Marketing is a process, not an event.

Your work will sell if you find the right buyer. And you can entice the right buyer to buy when you ensure:

- The quality and craftsmanship are superior
- Your design is exceptional in appearance and function
- The quality and price are commensurate with the value you deliver
- You market your wares where interested buyers will see, learn about and appreciate both you and your work

5

HOW DO I SET UP MY SHOP FOR THIS?

I n planning your shop layout, you should strive toward several diverse objectives: efficiency, safety, comfort and enjoyment. You will spend a great deal of time plying your craft, and your shop should meet those objectives.

This chapter contains some thoughts on your work flow system:

- Planning interior arrangement
- Procedures needed to make your product
- Shop plan and elevation views
- Work flows
- Production schedules
- Tool maintenance log
- Safety

SMART SETUPS THAT WORK

Efficient material-handling for the small shop may require only improving on how you have done things in your hobby, or an entirely new look at what you need to produce the desired level of quality in quantity, both safely and efficiently. A workable shop layout helps you achieve a higher level of both.

Lay out your shop for the work flow, the physical size of your shop and the products being worked. Adequate lighting, convenient power outlets, an efficient dust collection system, safe storage of volatile and flammable supplies, and all else that makes the process safer and more efficient are important.

The ideal shop

An ideal shop in an ideal world would have rooms or spaces dedicated exclusively for the following:

- **Lumber storage**—a dry area for boards and sheet stock stacked on end (assuming your shop has adequate ceiling height) or stored well-supported in horizontal bins or racks. Even outside storage may be OK with proper stacking to air-dry lumber that is sticked and stored. The storage area is directly in line where stock can be pulled from storage, positioned and cut to length on the radial arm or miter/cutoff saw.

- A cabinet saw, with ample extensions and supporting surfaces, is in a **cutting room** with plenty of space for feed and outfeed, maybe (even in the ideal space) through door openings when working on a whopping project.

- The cut lengths or glued-up parts are moved to the **rough milling area** with a thickness planer (if this step is a part of your process) and then the jointer/planer, shaper table, belt sander, spindle sander and all manner of tools used for your products.

- If your work involves wood bending, a **steamer** setup would be adjacent to the forming jigs for quick removal and forming while the wood is still pliable. Where gluing up boards, curves or other laminated forms, you set up a **glue pot** with all the clamps and jigs you need within reach to form the shapes. The ideal shop could include a curing area for these subassemblies to get them out of the way while new members are being laid up.

- The **kitting room** is where parts are sorted and stored adjacent to the assembly bench, ready for assembly.

- Finish machining and **surface preparation** is in a room with a good vacuum collection and air filtration system to collect the sanding dust.

- Your **spray booth** or brushing area is ultraclean, well-ventilated and away from the residue emanating from the other shop areas.

- And finally you can **warehouse** the finished goods, carefully packed and ready for the customer, or send them off your ample, truck-bed-high loading dock, on their way to a show.

Some of the profiled woodworkers' shops have reached or approached ideal. Their expanded facilities, however, did not drive early success. Instead the success of their products and marketing approach made their expansion possible. Their improved facilities pave the way for more efficient operation and future growth. Just to note, even the "ideal" facilities have revealed a few flaws discovered after the best plans were put to the test.

> "About the only thing I would do differently, if I had more money, would be to make my shop bigger, and this door needs to be 7′ wide instead of 6′ wide. I don't do cabinet work unless it's for me, and I don't do panels for anything very often, but you don't know where to put your saw so you can split a 4′ × 8′ sheet in half. By the time you add the molding, you have a 5′8″ or 5′6″ opening. It could be bigger. And I would like to have a bigger vacuum system. If I won the lottery tomorrow, I'd revacuum my entire shop while I screw around for a couple of months."—Randy Bader

A workshop in the real world

In the real world, all of the separate spaces listed above become separate operations performed in whatever common space you have to work with, whether this is working within the cramped confines of a small space under the basement stairs, a shared garage or a separate shop building.

There are some things you might consider to utilize the space most efficiently. Here are a few truisms:

1. As your business develops, you will soon discover bigger and meaner tools to add to your shop. Begin

planning your layout to accommodate future acquisitions. Be realistic about how much equipment will fit and still be accessible.

2. Electrical demands of a growing shop should be planned at the outset, maybe with the help of your electric company. Lighting should be on the plus side of adequate. Many well-grounded power outlets (duplex and quad) for your tools should be wired to the rating of the motors and local building codes and conveniently placed for trouble-free operation.

NAME: **Randy Bader**

LOCATION: **Laguna Beach, California**

PRODUCT: **Contemporary furniture and furnishings**

SINCE: **1980**

TRAINING: **M.A., Cal State Fullerton**

SHOP: **Designed and built shop and gallery loft in Laguna**

PRICING: **Retail almost exclusively**

AFFILIATIONS: **Exhibits in two shows in Laguna Beach: the Laguna Festival of the Arts and the Sawdust Festival. Both shows run concurrently each summer.**

Randy Bader built his shop/studio in Laguna Beach, California, a short distance up Laguna Canyon from the Sawdust Festival and the Laguna Festival of the Arts, the only festivals he shows each summer. He and a sculptor built the facility and each occupies one-half of the building.

Q What event launched your change to woodworking?

A I don't really consider myself a woodworker as much as I do an artist, or artisan or whatever—I didn't come from cabinetmaking. In 1973 I started taking art classes, and I wanted to do something no one had ever done—that's how naive I was—to make furniture that was art. I had no concept of what was being done. I got my bachelor's degree in 1978, and my master's of art in 1980. It was around that time I started doing the Sawdust Festival.

Q Who or what was most helpful?

A They didn't have a furniture program in college, but we had a jewelry teacher who allowed us to explore furniture and earn our master's degree in general craft. They didn't have anybody teaching woodworking, just had a jewelry teacher who was a very good artist. His teaching was valid, and he understood jewelry.

Q What was the most valuable skill or attribute you brought to the business?

A I was very focused. I wanted things that an artisan doesn't normally have—a house in Laguna Beach and a shop in Laguna Beach. I didn't want to rent either one; I wanted to own them. I worked long hours. During the first eight summers I would work 120 hours a week with no days off for three months to get ready for the Laguna shows.

Q What obstacles did you encounter?

A I did some street shows, and I tried the Harvest Festival one year, and I said, "This is a joke." You are competing with people who don't live in expensive areas. You've got artists from all around, and I live in Laguna Beach where my costs are significantly higher. I have been doing the two Festivals since the summer of 1980, and that's all I do.

Q What are your plans for growth?

A Friends who started out like I did now have six employees and their gross is about ten times my gross, but they never touch a saw. I'm the kid in the garage playing with toys, and that's what I want to do. I like making furniture.

Q When did you begin selling?

A I had a friend, a technical assistant at the college, who had two products that he had been making—cutting boards and a mirror—and I had some boxes I was doing, so we decided to do the Sawdust Festival together—cutting boards, boxes, mirrors, jewelry.

He bailed after the first year. It was a real rough venue. People didn't understand what we were doing 15 years ago—producing really fine cutting boards that were delicately laminated exotic and nonexotic woods.

I decided to do the Sawdust Festival alone the following year because I saw the immense potential of the show if you fine-tuned your market and if you understood who you are selling to, you could just gradually build up a base. I thought it would be a linear progression, but I didn't realize it would be more like an exponential progression if you were tenacious and just kept at it.

Q You sell directly retail. Do you do anything on spec?

A Everything is by commission only. The only time I may have pieces to sell is during these two shows because I have to put something in my booth. I wish I could figure a way to do these two shows without doing that . . . having two booths with an attractive display. This year I have two dining arm chairs, a dining table, a wall cabinet, a mirror, a rocker, another rocker, a coffee table, a sofa table, and another mirror all on display right now. To get that volume of work and continue doing my commission work—that's the nightmare. I basically have to shut down my shop for two months. My income fluctuates at that point. For two months I'm making pieces for the show.

The ideal situation might be to hold a preshow showing to previous clients to see if I could sell out the show before I even put anything in there. When I do the shows, it is very rare that anybody can take anything until the end of the summer. I don't make two rocking chairs so I can have a backup.

Q What do you consider most important in your product: quality, design, craftsmanship or pricing?

A I rely on only one thing for my design, and that is the human body. There is no one thing that is most important. Everything has to be brought to light. The price? The price is so arbitrary. I mean my rocking chair at a garage sale might be worth $100, and at the Festival it's worth $3000 to $5000. I heard a story yesterday of a guy who bought a Maloof rocking chair for $50 at a garage sale. So pricing is very arbitrary. Anybody who looks at others to set the price is always going to screw himself up.

I don't price my pieces with a penny to take off. I price them at what I think they are worth. If somebody says, "How about knocking a couple hundred bucks off that?" I say, "No." It's very rare, unless a good client sees one of my pieces that has been around for a while. I might offer it to him at a lower price. I won't barter with him. If someone comes up to me and says, "I can see that is a lot of work but it's not worth 1000 bucks." Right—you make it for $800 then. I price my stuff at the price I expect to sell it. I don't price it so I can lower it later. And I also believe that anybody who starts bartering has already decided they want to buy your piece. Most artisans/craftspeople, when they lower the price, are giving away money, because the guy's already decided, *This is a nice piece, the price is good, but let's see if I can get it for less.*

Q Do you operate your business as a sole proprietor?

A I'm the advertising man, the CEO, the CFO. I'm everything. I even do windows.

Q What percent increase have you seen from year to year in building your business?

A I never tried to build a business. I build furniture. My income doesn't go up part of the year and down part of the year. My backlog right now is between 5 to 15 months. So I just come down to the shop to work. When I was doing cutting boards my income went up every year. About the only way for me to make more money was to raise my prices.

Q Could you add help?

A Are you really going to make more money if you get help? You're going to slow down, first of all. When I was producing cutting boards, my hands were really healthy. I could produce about $120 per hour with the cutting boards. As soon as I hired someone, it went down to $35 per hour. I didn't do much of the work, and I only did it for one year. Unless you have a manager between you and your employees, the employees are the boss, not you. If they don't show up you've got to do their work. They come to work and you have to figure out something for them to do.

---

3. The size of some jobs—whether ceiling height; or the length of the ripping, resawing or thickness planing run; or just 4′ × 8′ sheets of ply or melamine cut for your shop or to put bread on the table—will always tax the setup. If large, long stock handling is routine in what you build, plan your shop layout accordingly. Otherwise, if the requirement is rare, you can be a little inconvenienced some of the time, opting for an efficient layout for the majority of your jobs.

4. At times shop doors will be slightly smaller or offset from where you would like them. Floor tools can be temporarily relocated to perform the occasional operation.

If starting fresh, inventory your major floor and bench tools, planning for tools you may acquire in the future. Then, on a sheet of grid paper, mark out the overall dimensions and cut out "footprints" of your floor tools, workbenches (and bench tools mounted on the workbench) to that same scale. Arrange and rearrange the tool cutouts to find the best layout for you and what you produce. Some objectives to keep in mind include:

- Adequate Clearances—feed, outfeed alignment and swing space for materials being worked
- Close Proximity—adjacent tools for sequential operations, or of hand tools, hold-downs, fences and guides
- Easy Access—to frequently used jigs, aids, parts
- Good Lighting—general illumination as well as task lights for close work on the tools or at the workbench
- Convenient outlets—power source for floor tools, for mounted bench tools and power hand tools both at the wall or center bench and power to the center bay

CHOOSING A NEW LOCATION OR MAKING DO WITH WHAT YOU HAVE

Review your existing tools and space. A fresh look at the layout, especially if you may be producing something of a different size, may show how you can improve upon your present setup.

If the selected site is on a floor and not on a concrete pad, maybe over a basement or crawl space, or in an attic, be sure the floor members will adequately bear the present and planned load of heavy and sometimes vibrating equipment, stored lumber and the throngs of customers who will be beating a path through your shop.

For what you produce, the shop might be your:

- kitchen table
- spare bedroom
- attached studio/shop
- basement workshop

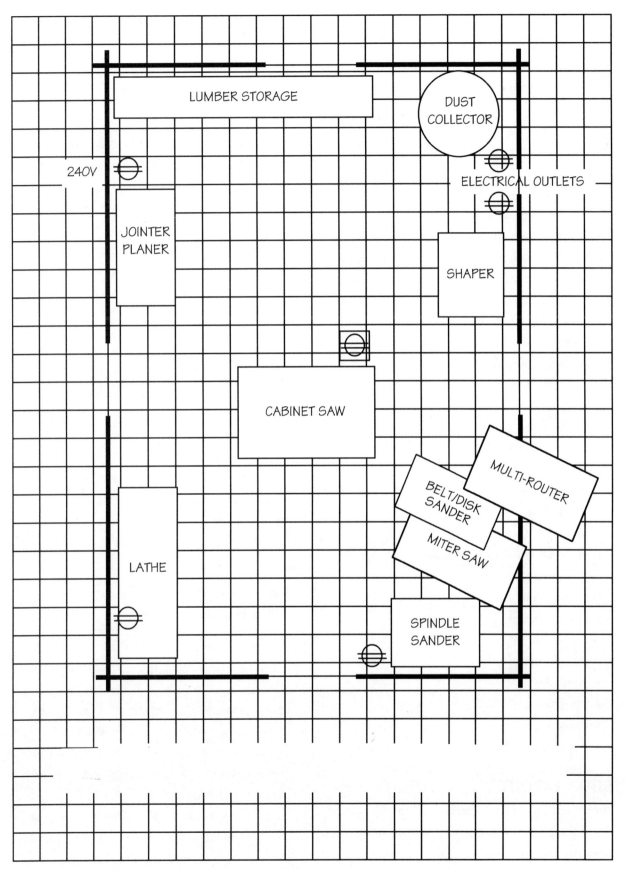

Figure 5-1 Planning the Shop Arrangement

- attached garage (shared)
- attached garage (no cars allowed)

Workshop spaces integral with the living quarters have both advantages and disadvantages:

Advantages

- Shared heating/electrical (if adequate)
- Short commute to work

Disadvantages

- Noise and vibration
- Fumes from glues and finishes
- Sawdust, both airborne and "footborne"

At the outset or later stages of your growth you might consider what type of square footage you will need and how this should be arranged for the products:

- **New shop location**

  A dedicated work shed

  An industrial park

  An artists/artisan complex

  Your own building
- **Shop layout and equipment**

  Single product

  Multiple products or variations

  Diverse products
- **Work flow**
- **Material storage**

  Stacking—air drying; keeping boards true

  Quantities—just-in-time inventory

  Dimensioned lumber
- **Parts fabrication**

  Rough-cut

  Rough milling
- **Assembly**
- **Pre-finishing**
- **Finishing**
- **Warehousing**

SHOP LAYOUT

Your layout should be designed for the frequent operations. Keep tools and supplies you use frequently, close and accessible.

A small production area changes function as the job progresses. Cutting jigs and fixtures lining the

Jon Sauer—Ornamental Turnings

A garage-based operation, Jon's garage in Pacifica, California, is filled with the tools of his trade: a few ornamental lathes and a rose engine machine. Both were invented and designed for milling material other than wood. The rose engine is a tool of engravers of fine watches, and the ornamental lathes were used to produce products from ivory. This equipment is antique, found in England. The remainder of his garage workshop houses his rough stock, his rough-milled turning blanks and a few boxes he can ship and set up at the call of a trade show.

Myron Van Ness—Ship Models

Myron's shop is a front bedroom in his Laguna Beach house, totally destroyed and rebuilt after a fire. Lost were his own ship models and his resource library among everything else more important, but not to this text. Myron works in miniature, and has opted for jeweler's type saws and drills (with drill bits from the dental trade).

Mark Allen—Arts and Crafts Furniture, Architectural Woodworking

Mark and a finish carpenter share space in an industrial park not far from Mark's source of work, the Laguna Festival of the Arts. They recently expanded into an adjacent bay, giving each a bit more room to work. The annex space is for lumber storage and rough milling operations. The main area has a central work island for assembling and finishing.

Their arrangement includes sharing rent and overhead on the shop and tools, plus reciprocal help when one of them is overloaded. Some commissions come from each other's customers.

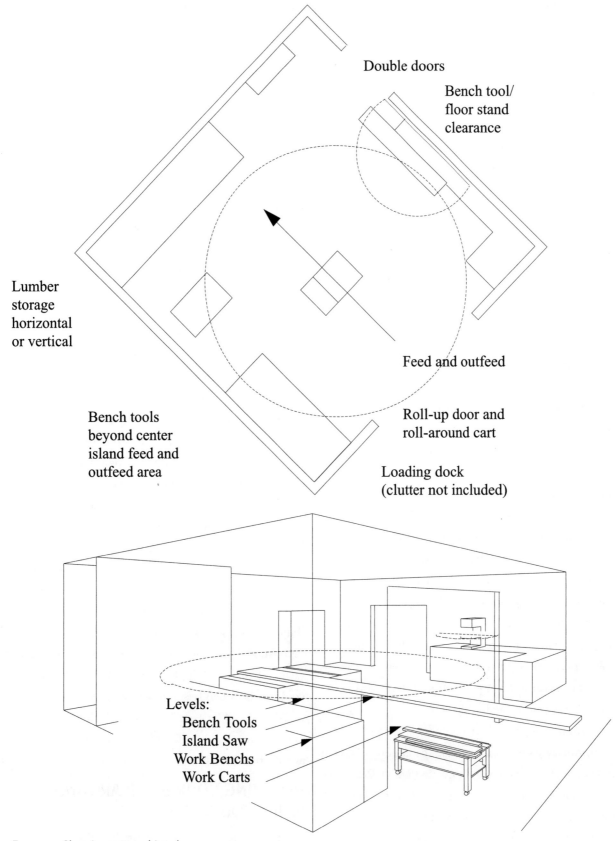

Double doors

Bench tool/
floor stand
clearance

Lumber
storage
horizontal
or vertical

Feed and outfeed

Bench tools
beyond center
island feed and
outfeed area

Roll-up door and
roll-around cart

Loading dock
(clutter not included)

Levels:
Bench Tools
Island Saw
Work Benchs
Work Carts

FIGURE 5-2 Shop Layouts and Levels

walls come out for that process. Workbenches, both stationary and mobile, are at or below table-saw height. Your nearby tools surrounding the cabinet saw or saw stand should also be positioned outside the width, length and throw of stock sizes you most often use. Occasionally some tools can be moved. If possible, your layout should accommodate 90 percent of the stock sizes you handle, even if you normally run a ripped board out the door.

In very cramped quarters, worktop heights or working levels are important considerations. Not having just fallen off a turnip truck, you will place the tall tools against a wall, well away from the interference of a milling operation. Bench tools can encroach into the feed/take-up zone, as long as they don't interfere with access and the travel of both yourself and the board being ripped, crosscut, planed or shaped.

From your general arrangement selected from the preliminary paper doll exercise, consider the layout (plan view) and the levels (elevation view). Rearrange shop tools in tight spaces to cross cut or rip long stock or to cut the plywood or melamine. These are infrequent tasks, so devoting enough clear floor space may not be practical or possible.

You can use lower-wheeled carts, portable stands for the outfeed rollers and saw tables and extensions that are slightly elevated from the permanent benches around the perimeter for more handling area without impeding the operation.

Electrical

On your plan arrangement, begin laying out your electrical needs. Two circuits—one for the lights and one for the tools—should feed your workshop or shop area. The lights can operate on a lower amperage (say a 15-ampere circuit) and will stay on if the tool circuit (at 20 amperes) overloads and trips the power supply. Two circuits of 15 amps may be enough, as long as only one tool is running at a time. With multiple drain, their total draw should not exceed 15 amps. If this trips the breaker or blows a fuse, a higher rated circuit or an additional circuit is needed. Using a higher rated fuse can overload and overheat the wires beyond their safe capacity.

A master switch on the tool circuit is a good idea. Locate it well above the reach of curious children.

Local electrical codes will govern how you or an electrician wire the shop. The two dedicated circuits will come off your main power panel or a separate panel installed for the shop. Your electric company will help determine if your service is sufficient to power your workshop, or whether another line or maybe a larger service box is required.

Lay out the electrical plan providing power to the electric tool locations, dust collection systems and maybe an electric heater. Overhead lights for general illumination, again on a separate circuit, can be wired in, or shop lights can be plugged into overhead receptacles. If you use a duplex box to do this, a short drop cord can be a handy source of power for power hand tools in a middle bay. Be sure to include sufficient outlets for task lights (if not built into your machinery) at workbench height.

PLANNING YOUR SHOP AROUND WHAT YOU MAKE

Developing a system flow

There is some order to how you have set up your shop, regardless of what any onlooker says. Tools are placed where the operations are performed and where the materials can be swung and fed and worked, all under adequate lighting, ventilation and dust collection ducts.

A work flow pattern has developed for the products you make. Rough milling of rough stock produces the blanks or pieces to be further shaped into their final form and then finished and readied for delivery. Shaping, for your product, may entail steam bending, laminating or machining. Space and equipment are selected for the operations performed and the size and quantities worked during each step.

New tools, oh boy!

New tools, like new facilities, do not beget success; they result from the success. With a few exceptions noted in the profiles, most professional woodworkers ease into new tool purchases, unless it is critical to start-up or initial business growth.

But if you have determined that the production costs can be greatly decreased with the addition of a special tool, go for it. Maybe you're spending more money on surfaced lumber, and the quantities justify buying your own thickness planer (for rough-sawn lumber) or adding a band saw (for resawing to the needed thickness). A popular tool of the profiled artisans is a multi-router, which can do in a morning what might take a week if doing mortises and tenons by hand. A spindle sander is critical if your designs tend to be flowing, arcing forms. If the profit potential is assured, and you have crunched the numbers, it may be time to bring in new or refurbished tools.

Tool buyer's guides from woodworking magazines or maybe even *Consumer Reports* are a handy place to start shopping. Check with your local woodworker's supply houses and ask other craftspeople to gain insight into what is good and what works. Magazine ads are also a place to begin, as are woodworking tool and equipment shows.

Quality of the tools is reflected in the quality of your product and the time it takes to produce it. Remember, too, that the hobbyist may spend only a few hours a week in the workshop, which barely begins to break in the tools made for that market. The professionals may put their equipment to the test daily, so the stamped metal frames should (and will) give way to maybe an older model of cast metal parts. If the motor powering a tool is lower rated, any load will soon take it to its electrical knees. Lots of amps and excess power capacity will prolong the tool's useful life. Buy tools close to industrial grade, which offer adequate power and capacity.

Also, cast or even machined surfaces for hobby tools may not be as precise as you will need. Vernier scales of angles and alignment of blades to miter guides are critical for the type of joinery you and your clients expect.

Once a used piece of equipment has been refurbished, which may require resurfacing pitted tables, replacing shafts and bearings or rebuilding a motor, the life of a hefty product will be long and prosperous.

Material storage and handling

You can store and prepare large quantities of stock in a small space. Material sources and buying materials are discussed in chapter six. For now, we are interested in how you store what you buy.

Your inventory of lumber will vary with the types and quantities of jobs in progress. And you may want to stockpile choice pieces of woods when you find them, before you have a need for them. Whether you buy and store rough-sawn or milled stock, how much quantity you keep on hand depends on the space you can allocate to lumber storage. Many businesses far larger than yours are reducing their materials storage space and handling by opting instead to buy as needed—the just-in-time purchasing philosophy.

If it's a day trip to your lumberyard, you will want to stockpile more than if your supplier is close and you can conveniently drop in and select superior quality stock that is adequately stored.

Vertical versus horizontal storage is a matter of your viewpoint and an adequate ceiling height for the lengths needed. Horizontal wall racks are an efficient

NAME: **Mark Allen**

LOCATION: **Laguna Beach, California**

PRODUCT: **Arts and Crafts furniture and architectural woodworking**

SINCE: **1979**

TRAINING: **Self-taught**

SHOP: **Shares shop in Laguna Beach with Dave Lincoln, a finish carpenter. Their association nets referrals from each other's specialty.**

PRICING: **Retail commissions**

AFFILIATIONS: **Exhibits in the annual Laguna Festival of the Arts. Customer referrals.**

Mark Allen shares shop space with a finish carpenter. Each works independently, but each refers his clients to the other, and they sometimes collaborate on large architectural projects. This facility in an industrial complex is also near the Laguna Festival of the Arts, where he shows his work exclusively. Mark's approach to buying better used machinery and refurbishing it is a tandem story.

Q **What event launched your change to woodworking?**

A It pretty much started when I bought my home in 1979. I didn't like the furniture I saw out there. So I bought some tools and built my own, which was, in some respects, a mistake because it evolved to where I'm at now. I enjoy woodworking, but there can be frustrations.

Q **Who or what was most helpful?**

A I took a few classes at Saddleback College mainly to use their tools. The instruction wasn't that helpful. Originally I didn't have that many tools. They had a nice big jointer, so I would go in there to use the jointer to build doors. I scheduled the projects to the fit work I was doing at that time, and it worked out well.

Q **What was the most valuable skill or attribute you brought to the business?**

A I think my eye for detail and my desire to produce the highest quality work—being my toughest critic. Knowing you have just completed a piece that you're proud enough to put your name on it, and that the client will be happy with it.

Q **What obstacles did you encounter?**

A I had few tools and was working out of my garage. I built some pieces that I look back on now and see that they were terrible. But people started asking me to make things for them.

Q **What are your plans for growth?**

A Financially I've never had enough money to really market myself, although I know it is important. There are a number of avenues you can take, like magazine advertising. I would focus on a couple of Arts and Crafts-style magazines. But then you have to build something in quantity that can be shipped—and to do that, you almost have to get beyond the custom, one-man shop.

Q **How would you classify your design style?**

A Pretty much Arts and Crafts style is what I do. Stickley and Greene and Greene seem to be most popular. I recently completed a Frank Lloyd Wright dining room set and some bar stools.

The original Stickley furniture—people think that furniture was the ultimate—was made for the masses. Basic simple style, no ornamentation, and you would pay $20 to $100 for it, totally restored. In the late eighties you couldn't give that stuff away. They used to buy lots of furniture and it was always a bunch of Stickley stuff. If it was broken, it wasn't worth fixing. You would salvage some parts and use them for other pieces of furniture. Today there is a market for Arts and Crafts.

Q Were these commissioned or on spec?

A It's almost all commissioned work. I have some proven designs I show clients and we're able to come up with a variation instead of designing the thing again. I can pretty much suit their needs.

Q In addition to the Laguna Festival of the Arts, where do you showcase your work?

A I've done a couple other shows. The art show at the La Quinta Resort in the desert near Indio (California), and I did the Beverly Hills show a few times. But I discovered that transporting furniture to shows like that isn't worth the risk of damage, even though the desert show did real well.

Q Do you wholesale your work or sell retail?

A I pretty much deal directly with customers. But I've worked with a few interior designers and architects over the years. In addition to furniture, I build doors, windows and other architectural things.

Q What percentage of the business is from architectural jobs?

A It really varies. Overall, probably 20 percent. The shop is set up to do both the furniture and architectural work. I've got an old hollow chipper/mortiser and a single end tenoner. All the joinery here is mortise and tenon type construction.

Q How would you rank the order of importance of quality, design, craftsmanship and pricing?

A Quality? Number one. Design—it was a good call to follow the Arts and Crafts style—I would rate that as number one, and craftsmanship is definitely number one.

I don't know how to rate pricing for the style of furniture I build. And I guess other custom builders as well would like to get them more affordable, but I really won't give up quality or craftsmanship. If the buyer is looking for price, there are places to buy things that are less expensive.

Q Are you operating as a sole proprietor or a partnership?

A As a sole proprietor, but Dave Lincoln and I share the space. He's a finish carpenter. We work together on some furniture and architectural-type commissions.

If there is a door job in here, there are a lot of things two guys can be doing and not get in the way of each other. But custom furniture is a one-man deal. I may bring in part-time help to sand and that kind of thing. It's hard to justify doing that yourself, although I do it 90 percent of the time.

Dave had been working on a Craftsman-style home, and we were asked to do the furniture. We did it on a time-and-material basis. For a lot of custom furniture that is almost a prerequisite. That is a good way, and you can set down in a contract that it will not go over X amount.

Q Without divulging income, what kind of year-to-year growth have you experienced?

A I really haven't grown. Business has remained steady.

Probably in the late eighties I was making more than I'm making now, but I was doing more architectural-type work. Whenever you can build multiples of something, your profit margin is much better than building one or two, which typically is what custom furniture is going to be.

Since that time I've been staying steady doing something in the shop—furniture 90 percent of the time, and architectural work. We'll get two or three door jobs a year from contractors we've worked with over the years.

Q **What is one bit of encouragement for somebody that wants to launch their own woodworking business?**

A Buy the best equipment you can afford. There is a great used market out there if you know where to look and have some patience. The cost of tooling up can be fairly expensive and gets more so after people find the faults in their tools after they've already bought them.

And there are things besides equipment. It's going to take years before anybody is going to feel confident and capable of going out there and making money. I look back on what I did, and even though people were asking me to make things for them, I didn't feel qualified. I guess it has been 12 years since I considered myself full-time—really since I have been doing the Arts and Crafts furniture.

use of space and, if fully supported between braces, keep the lumber flat and true. Without a support between widely spaced braces, the lumber could develop a permanent slump between supports. Vertical storage may encourage a latent potential to twist or cup, especially in green or unseasoned lumber.

Many factors can affect the integrity of the wood you buy and how you store it. Green lumber, from logs to milled boards, will lose water content and continue to shrink and swell depending on the surrounding temperature and humidity. You should initially buy long in the event of end splitting and checking. Before storing, you might be wise to cut off the questionable ends to stop any continued cracking. Find a place to pile and stick very green lumber so air can circulate between the pieces to deter rotting or fungus growth.

Air-dried lumber, and even kiln-dried lumber, will react to the ambient conditions and should be stored indoors. Inspect the ends, trim if necessary and seal the end grain with a coat of shellac or carnauba wax.

For horizontal storage, depending on the quantity and lengths required, consider:

1. Storage along a lower shelf in a long workbench.

2. Wall-mounted brackets and braces attached along the wall to exposed studs.

3. Wooden or metal floor racks built to the depth, length and height to match the lengths and the space the lumber occupies.

4. Overhead frames suspended from a high open-beam and rafter roof. Design for and maintain safe load limits.

5. Lumber shed as a lean-to along an outer wall, or a long and narrow structure with an opening into the shop.

SHOP MAINTENANCE

Strategies for keeping on top of tool use and maintenance include, "If it ain't broke, don't fix it." But there are things you should do to make sure it stays "ain't broke." Keeping motors free of accumulated sawdust is a matter of brushing or vacuuming out the debris. Keeping tools dry and protecting equipment from the elements (even humidity) means an occasional rubbing out with steel wool and a penetrant. Lubricating bearings, checking and dressing pulley

TOOL MAINTENANCE LOG

Tool: _____

Serial Number: _____

Operation	Frequency	Dates Completed	Notes
Lubrication Schedule			
Vacuum and Brush			
Sharpening			
Surface Protection			
Tool Sharpening			
Belt Inspection and Dressing			
Motor Housing Heating			
Shaft Drag			
Check and Clean or Replace Filters			

Tool Maintenance Log

belts and performing other maintenance ensures the machinery will be operative when you need it.

SHOP SAFETY AND ERGONOMICS

A workshop is an accident waiting to happen. You should always consider and be alert to such issues as:

- Proper grounding of all electrical equipment
- Respect for potentially hazardous equipment
- Use of guards on pulleys, pulley belts and discs
- Use of hold-downs and push sticks
- Wear safe clothing with nothing to catch in equipment
- Protective goggles, ear protection, proper mask
- Adequate lighting
- Good dust collection system

If you have a shop of employees you'll also need to become familiar with:

OSHA—You can do yourself in, but don't mess with employees.

MSDS—Keep Material Safety Data Sheets on file for all chemicals used in the operation.

Products to keep you safe:

- Dust collecting system
- Protection—eyes, ears, hands
- Rubber mats
- Castored stools

Don't forget to abide by common sense safety rules:

- Keep guards in place.
- Don't operate power tools while fatigued.
- No loose clothing.
- Use pushers and hold-downs.

Chemical storage is another important concern. Be careful when using or storing toxic/noxious and combustible materials.

- Take note of chemical flash points and take measures to avoid reaching them.
- Use only approved storage containers.
- Dispose of chemical impregnated rags properly.

6

How Do I Make and Keep My Business Profitable?

The previous chapter addressed how to set up your shop for efficiency. This chapter provides some tips on setting up the business side of your business effectively. Sharpen both your shop tools and financial management tools to tackle subjects ranging from budgeting, cost analysis, cost containment to filling the pipeline with product and customers.

What return do you need to make from your woodworking business? This section looks at how to evaluate your business potential as an investment. What kind of return can you expect on the capital you invest in your woodworking business? How will you increase your returns from your woodworking business?

At this point you should have:
- Financial objectives clearly stated
- Product and market in balance
- Costs known and target prices set
- Production facility equipped

FINANCIAL RECORDS

Few beginning businesspeople/artisans will have the time to both produce and to track results in the detail shown in these examples, but you will somehow keep aware of your costs, operating margins and cash flow without preparing a set of formal financial reports. At some point in the future, more formal records may be necessary for obtaining outside financing or just knowing the progress and worth of the business you have built.

By definition, accounting for business finances is:
- Bookkeeping—recording and summarizing business transactions
- Cost Accounting—cost of goods sold—direct ma-

terials, direct labor, overhead (both direct and the burden of the operation)
- Financial Accounting—financial statements

Rapid growth makes record keeping critical, *and* it can divert your attention and time away from that activity. Maintaining accurate records provides you with information to help you succeed and avert failure, or even insolvency. Prolonged periods of negative cash flow may make you unable to pay creditors. Having too much debt or heavy inventory or accounts receivable can "get you into a pickle." Your up-to-date records will alert you to such situations before they become problems.

Good record keeping is an essential part of tracking your business. Five categories of records every business should have are:
- Sales—gross proceeds from sales
- Income Log—source, item, date and amount received
- Cost of Sales—direct costs by unit sold
- Net Income—sales less cost of sales by unit, by total
- Cash Flow—positive or negative cash flow by period

These figures can be kept in a basic transaction journal: receipts, disbursements, sales, purchases. Also keep a record of your inventory and accounts receivable and payable.

CASH CONVERSION

The product you bring to market accumulates expenses during design, production and shipping that you do not recoup until you receive proceeds from the item's sale, at the completion of the product cycle.

A typical product cycle comprises the:

- outlay for raw materials
- investment in shop equipment
- value of your time (and that of any helpers) in production
- cost (time and money) of marketing, sales and delivery

Cash conversion cycle duration

The longest duration of cash outlay is forever, never to see it return. This can be intentional when making samples and prototypes for promotion and for generating other sales. It can be unintentional if what you built on spec doesn't sell. These false starts can be recorded and written off to experience.

When selling to an end user, cash is usually received on delivery. Commissioned work (at the retail level) can include progress payments that allow you to use the customer's capital throughout the production of the piece. Better still, a deposit (which is customary) allows you to use the up-front cash for materials, and progress payments by agreement can be made along the way. This is particularly important in large jobs of long duration.

Working on a backlog of firm orders also defines the duration of the cash conversion cycle, which is partially determined by your dates of completion and delivery. However, the cash conversion cycle continues beyond the sale of your item until you receive the proceeds, which, if allowed, could occur well beyond the date of sale. To minimize this gap, specify your payment policy in dealings or contracts with clients.

Wholesaling to shop owners should follow the direct retail cycle, but they too are concerned with cash flow and may push the 30-day payment agreement into 60 or 90 days. Be firm in your policy, and maybe offer a ½-percent discount for prompt payment. Consigning, rather than wholesaling, your product to a shop owner could result in a lengthy, open-ended cash conversion cycle. The likelihood of shortening that cycle is greater when consigning to a proven retailer who has moved your work before.

Cash flow

An item in inventory or consigned to a retailer represents tied-up cash. Work in progress ties up cash, both in cost of goods sold (direct manufacturing costs of materials and labor) and the operating costs of the facility.

The cash conversion cycle of a single unit of a single design is easy to define. For example, let's assume for Design A, Unit 1 your costs are $100. As the table on page 86 illustrates, the cash flow would be negative until the receipt of sale proceeds.

A hobbyist may commit resources to produce one item at a time and sell that item at a $20 profit that is then used to buy materials for the next item. The same applies to large commissioned pieces; just add a few zeros to the cost examples.

A business has a pipeline that needs to be kept filled and flowing. The clarity of the cash conversion cycle becomes a little blurred by staggered schedules and delayed proceeds.

From the simple example on page 87, you can see your cash flow at any point during the production cycle and see your negative and positive cash flow positions. As you add more units of the same and other designs you may lose the string, especially when other variables creep into the flowchart. Materials bought in quantity for a better price are bought sooner than needed for a unit to be produced later. This adds cash outlays earlier, but reduces unit costs by the discount you earned. During the middle of the cycle, the production process may take more man-hours than estimated, or more time than planned may be necessary to bring it to market. The wholesaler or direct retail customer may then take 30, 60 or even 90 days to remit payment.

Well-maintained records showing revenues when received and expenses when incurred track these numbers in aggregate amounts, as shown in table 6-1.

Cash flow shows the sources and uses of cash

NAME: **Salvatore Maccarone**
LOCATION: **Port Townsend, Washington**
PRODUCT: **Sculpture, furniture, glass**
SINCE: **1971**
TRAINING: **Master's degree in sculpture. Apprenticed.**
SHOP: **1500-sq. ft. workshop and showroom**
PRICING: **100 percent retail: one-half commercial, one-half private**
AFFILIATIONS: **Self-promotes by word of mouth and Internet home page. Publishes articles. Author of *Tune Up Your Tools*, Betterway Books, 1996.**

Sal Maccarone actively seeks out new opportunities through both commercial and privately commissioned work. He participates in designing the environs for his custom furniture, sculpture and glass and garners the resources and help needed to produce. Sal continues to build on a solid business background, and he even operated (and sold) a chain of profitable retail stores.

Q **What event launched your full-time woodworking venture?**

A Key projects. I did a restaurant in the San Francisco Bay area (in Los Gatos) that got my name front and forward. I spent a number of years surviving, so to speak, and all of a sudden I landed this commercial project that involved an old Victorian bar among other things. It seemed like the minute that place opened, people woke up to the fact that I was around. From that point on, the business just took off. That was probably 2½ years into my career. Up to that point I was doing run-of-the-mill type things, literally—cabinets and other mainstay types of woodworking.

Q **Who or what was most helpful?**

A I had the unique privilege, while working on my master's degree at San Jose State, of serving a three-year apprenticeship to an internationally famous sculptor, Sam Richardson. He didn't teach me much to do with technique, but he sure had a lot to do with attitude. I guess it was then and there that I learned what art, per se, was all about. I like to think that I come from an art background. It all pertains to woodworking. I worked for $2 an hour, which was insignificant. I wasn't there for the money. I had a thirst for attitude, and he really helped me out in that regard, and it stuck with me.

Q **What was the most valuable skill or attribute you brought to the business?**

A I would have to think communication, which really has nothing to do with the business, but it is a people-oriented business—at least what I do. I pride myself on being able to do what the client wants, and in order to do that, you need to get into their personalities.

Q **What obstacles have you encountered in your business?**

A An obstacle may be distance—the inability to visit the property and having to work from photographs, which is fine, but I'm not able to spend as much time with the person.

For instance, I'm working on a project in New York, and it's logistically impossible to be over there as much as I want. I did visit it once and got a real good sense of the client at that point. I like to visit the property as much as I possibly can, especially the bigger commercial projects.

Q For your private business, do you sell direct or through galleries?

A I don't do anything with galleries. When I first started out, I did a little, and I found that as a marketing tool it's OK, but they want to make more money than you do. That's been my experience. Everybody's in business to make money; there's no doubt about that. But this work is very laborious. There are hours and hours of work that go into it. I just carved myself a little niche, and I market myself—primarily through my commercial projects. My work is all over the country. Not too terribly much local. It never has been. I target the upper one percentile of the population—those who can afford it.

Q Your claim to fame is the bar you built.

A That's one of the claims. That bar was in a property called Marriott Tenaya Lodge in Mariposa, California, near where I lived. I have done a lot of work for Marriott. I'm in their library of designers. They've been one of my mainstays for years. It is a wonderful opportunity to work all over the country, and actually some internationally, making lobby pieces.

That bar took me six months. I had to build a building to build that in. It was really large. My shop at that time was 8' high, and the bar was 19' high, so I had to build a little annex to the studio 40' square, 10½' high just to do this project.

Q How do you get your name out?

A Different ways. On the commercial stuff, I have a little metal signature plate that I inlay on the underside of my pieces. For instance, I put my nameplate in a lobby table at a Marriott, so if somebody is inquisitive and looks around to see who made the darned thing, they'll find it.

Another way I market myself is on the Internet. I've got a website (http://www.waypt .com/maccarone/woodwork.htm). There I have a full portfolio and a description of what I do.

Q How many hits have you had?

A I've had quite a few hits, actually (number-wise, probably 5000 in the last six months). I'm real careful; that's how I spend my free time. Instead of watching TV, I'll get on the Internet looking for like pages that are willing to link me, and oftentimes I trade links to do that. For instance, I'll tap into designers, I'll tap into construction people, art, whatever might fit the bill. I try to get myself linked to as many things as I can and it seems to work.

Q So you sell directly to the buyer?

A I go to the individual who is ultimately going to own it. It is all commissioned work. It is all sold before it is made, and I require a deposit when I begin. Nothing on spec. I'll do a few pieces here and there when I get an idea. For instance, I just built a piece that had a lot of copper in it—remnants left over from a copper ceiling that I did for this Victorian house here in Port Townsend. I dreamed up a way to use them in a piece of furniture, and it turned out quite nice. It is in my showroom attached to the studio.

Q What is the mix of furniture in your showroom?

A I try to do as much as I can in my own style, which happens to be multispecies pieces, where I'll make a piece that is cherry with some accent of walnut, something that contrasts, but understated as much as I can. Recently, there has been a desire for French Provincial, and I have been doing quite a bit of that. Whatever is in vogue. It seems to go in trends. For a long time it was Victorian.

Q In what you produce, how would you rank quality, design, craftsmanship, delivery and pricing in order of importance?

A I wrote "Attitude for All Woodworkers" for *Popular Woodworking*—in the "Out of the Woodwork" section— and in there I spell out my attitude to do with woodworking. They are all important.

Q You are operating as a sole proprietor?

A Yes. Of course my retail stores operated as a corporation, and that's got its merits. But for what I'm doing, I'm pretty much the ringleader, and I don't see any reason to incorporate.

Q Is there a limit to how much you can make?

A There's a ceiling. I guess it depends on what aspect you get into. I've always stayed within the craftsmanship aspect. I had several opportunities in my career to go on and set up factories and have other people do the work, but I've always steered clear from that. I would rather be in there, hands-on.

When you are the guy making all the stuff, there is only so much you can do. And you don't want to price yourself out of the market. Fortunately, I get top dollar and couldn't justify getting much more. For instance, an armoire—I do probably 15 to 20 a year—is in the $3000 range. My work is priced in the range where you could go into a commercial furniture store and buy a particleboard rendition. Several people are making money off that—several layers of markup. The customer is going to pay about the same price, but the piece itself is worth only about $500.

That's kind of the rule of thumb. Don't be too ridiculous or you won't have work. So I always keep busy. I rate myself at about $40 to $46 an hour. That's what I try to make. That's more than enough.

PERIOD	1	2	3	4
Design Unit	Materials	Labor	Delivery	Sale
A 1	-$ 20	-$ 70	-$ 10	+ $120
Cumulative	-$ 20	-$ 90	-$100	+ $ 20

during an accounting period. A positive cash flow occurs when more cash comes in than goes out, and the opposite is true for a negative cash flow. Both may be present in the production cycle, but it is wise to monitor and evaluate both magnitude and duration, especially when operating with a negative cash flow for extended periods.

"One of my greatest fears is to run out of cash. Two most important elements of running a business are profit and cash flow, and if you don't pay attention to both of them they can kill you . . . they can put you out of business."—Jonathan Simons (see profile in chapter seven)

Even if your business is healthy and net assets exceed liabilities, you could face difficulties meeting current obligations if you're not generating enough cash to cover expenses. You may want to set up a cash budget, identifying future receipts and disbursement schedules on a weekly or monthly cycle. This is your cash conversion cycle—how long between the time

PERIOD	1		2		3		4		5
Design Unit									
A 1	Mat'ls -$ 20		Labor -$ 70		Dlvry -$ 10		Sale +$120		
A 2		Mat'ls -$ 20		Labor -$ 70		Dlvry -$ 10		Sale +$120	
A 3			Mat'ls -$ 20		Labor -$ 70		Dlvry -$ 10		Sale +$120
Cost by Month	-$ 20	-$ 20	-$ 90	-$ 70	-$ 80	-$ 10	+$110	+$120	+$120
Cumulative Cash Flow	-$ 20	-$ 40	-$130	-$200	-$280	-$290	-$180	-$ 60	+$ 60

you commit cash for raw materials to the time the money, including your profit, is returned after the sale of the product.

OPERATING INCOME

In addition to cash flow, which is a cash-position barometer, other historical numbers need to be kept and referenced when preparing tax statements and estimating costs for new work or new products.

Business records

A ledger type checkbook allows you to key revenue (deposits) and expense (checks) transactions to their dates.

"A chart of accounts may be in spreadsheet format, built from the checkbook ledger. It provides a more complete breakdown of costs by category by calendar period. The purpose here is to categorize expenses for tax time, and to record income (along with expenses) for a look at the finances. Your tax preparer will be happy to help set up the accounts so that tax time is less taxing for all.

A chart of accounts in a calendar spreadsheet format can tally gross revenue and expenses by month, and therefore be a cash flow indicator. Adding across in rows will sum whatever categories you set up to see where you are spending the money. This is an aid to you or your accountant in accumulating like items of expenses and income.

You may also consider assigning a product code to what you make and sell. Using job numbers and product codes facilitates a system of accountability and ease of accumulating income and expenses by job or product.

All costs and revenues associated with one product, or one line, or even a client identifier can be readily pulled out and evaluated individually. These figures provide a profit analysis by product or customer that could indicate the need to adjust price, adjust production costs or change the target market.

The use of a computer is a great help in building spreadsheets. An even easier way to keep cash accounting records is through a financial application software program. Whether you use the check-writing feature or not, you can still record the business information and produce a number of reports. Quicken, Quicken Quick-Books, Microsoft Money, or more sophisticated application programs, including Peachtree, that you and your accountant can share can help in the planning, the pricing and projecting growth. The cyberspace discussion in chapter two contains a few Internet addresses and toll-free numbers.

	PERIOD 1	PERIOD 2	PERIOD 3
Beginning Balance	$800	-$380	$540
Cash Receipts:			
Collections	300	2100	800
Interest	10	10	10
Financing	10	10	10
Total Receipts	320	2120	820
Disbursements:			
Operating Expenses	-500	-500	-500
Direct Labor Costs	-500	-200	-300
Cost of Materials	-250	-250	-400
Manufacturing Overhead	-250	-250	-250
Long-Term Debt	0	0	0
Interest Expense	0	0	0
Total Disbursements	-1500	-1200	-1450
Net Cash Flow	-1180	920	-630
Ending Balance	-$380	$540	-$ 90

TABLE 6-1 Cash Flow

"The business is in the black, always. It has always made its own way. I try not to borrow money, although I sometimes have to use a credit card, but I try to keep a real tight watch on it. You have to, or it gets away from you."—Dean Douglas

Operating budgets

Financial data collected over time become the basis for a realistic operating budget, which is a financial planning tool that supports business decisions. A cookie jar can be used to set aside funds budgeted for a purchase or purpose. A computer jockey will find a business or home finance software application program helpful in creating and maintaining a budget. At start-up, an individual may want to include household expenses in the budget as well, since the cash resources may have to provide for both the business and a subsistence.

Quicken, Microsoft Money, et al. automatically accumulate expenses against account codes for some prior time period—a quarter, a half year or a year—and sum income and expense amounts as a beginning for the budgeting exercise. You can edit the arithmetic to include changes to the historical income and expenses, e.g., removing a onetime expense that may not recur or adding budget for those purchases you plan in the future. Sales projections can be added to the current or past year to forecast anticipated sales growth from a price increase, a marketing push or a new product.

"I try to keep current on my costs. I have a good history of hours and expenses, and I apply these

NAME: **Dean Douglas**

LOCATION: **Albuquerque, New Mexico**

PRODUCT: **Willow stick furniture and accessories**

SINCE: **1983**

TRAINING: **M.A., University of Montana. House builder.**

SHOP: **1300 sq. ft. with 12′ ceilings**

PRICING: **Wholesale, retail, consignment**

AFFILIATIONS: **Shows at one local holiday craft fair a year, consigns to local galleries, wholesales to a few galleries nationwide, advertises in area visitor guide magazines**

He has always operated his one-man business in the black, watches cash flow closely, and only commits to as much business as he can produce.

Dean Douglas is a craftsman who works alone offering a niche product, Southwestern furniture and furnishings, from his workshop in Albuquerque, New Mexico.

Q What event launched your change to woodworking?

A I had always been interested in art, and I consider woodworking art. And I have always been interested in the way things work, in sculpture and three-dimensional things. I built houses for a while. And suddenly one day I had a shop, and here I am in the furniture business.

Q What obstacles did you encounter?

A Gathering together enough tools and meeting the rent. The cost of renting was high, but while it took a long time, I was able to buy my own building. Now my home and shop are on the same property. On some days I don't even need to start the truck.

Q What are your plans for growth?

A I don't have a hard schedule. I like to think about new things. A friend and I have a dialogue going. Alex is a woodworker too, and we talk about ways things could go. We're talking about making birdcages out of willow or salt cedar sticks. Willow is a beautiful stick in its natural state, and I think it would make quite an interesting dove cage.

Q Did you plan to be a woodworker?

A No, I slipped into woodworking. I was teaching for a while at the University of Montana, but that was too far away from the woodwork/art end of things. I have a bachelor's degree from the University of New Mexico and a master's in art from the University of Montana.

Q You have been billed as a willow stick woodworker. What is your specialty?

A Probably accent pieces, if I had one. Most of what I do is custom work right now, and most everything is ordered or commissioned. I have several products I make to fill repeat orders from galleries. Sometimes people will come in with an idea of what they want. I try to give them what they want if it's at all possible, but sometimes people's dreams don't work out.

Q Are these consigned pieces? Are you taking custom orders? Do you both wholesale and retail?

A As it works out I do both. I wholesale a bit. If somebody wants a big order I will wholesale to them. A gallery in Florida buys things from me on that basis. Then I consign some things to galleries here in Albuquerque, and I sell directly to customers.

Q How many gallery outlets do you use?

A One in Florida, and one in Colorado that I deal with, and one in Albuquerque. I had one in Santa Fe for a while, but I don't even know if it's still there. I haven't heard from them for so long.

Q Of those galleries, is there one that really moves your work?

A The local one in Albuquerque, by far. It varies, but over the year I probably do about 30 percent of my volume through them. Actually I get a lot of work from all over the country. I get orders from Kentucky, and I just filled some orders in Pennsylvania and am sending stuff to Arizona. It seems like I have a lot of work that comes from out of state.

Q Do you attribute that to the gallery exposure?

A Some to the gallery. But from time to time I will advertise in a magazine, and I think that works (and some advertising seems to have a long life). The latest one is an art magazine, *Abode*. That issue profiled work of different local craftsmen and artisans. The ad lasts a long time, more than a year or maybe two. It's a free magazine distributed through hotels, stores and galleries.

Q Have you considered using craft shows and wood shows at all as an outlet for your work?

A Several years ago, back when I had a business-partner, we did almost every craft show that came along. For two years running, we showed a lot, and that turned out to be too much work. I have slowly reduced it to where I do one show a year—one Christmas show in November. That's all I can really handle. My time is really filled. I have to be careful about what I'm getting into because I'm looking ahead for a whole year.

The Christmas show is retail; it is a large show at the Albuquerque Fairgrounds. I don't see immediate results, but people see my work year after year, and some time later on come back and order what they want. I always show a few things there. I'm getting referrals out of that.

Q Do you have walk-in business?

A I have a large workshop, but no showroom at the present time. Customers that come here usually call beforehand, and I warn them that they are coming to a working shop. I do have a portfolio to show.

Q How would you rank quality, design, craftsmanship and pricing?

A I make a quality product that is more expensive than the average piece because it requires longer to make. And that is about the only place that I found I can compete. I can't compete with mass-produced things at all, but I can compete on the value and on the design. I try to use my degree in art and past training, which I use along with my woodworking skills.

Q What kind of year-to-year sales increase have you experienced?

A I'm always trying to increase the quality of the product, which increases sales, but sometimes I do work that's not exactly along business lines. I refinished a walnut floor, which I don't usually do, but the customer insisted. I would much rather be creating my own designs, but I don't know how you can eliminate those fill-in kinds of jobs and still keep sales growing.

Q Do you have any ambitions of opening a gallery?

A I would love to. I was gallery director at the University of Montana. For two years I did nothing but shows, and that was fun. That was while I was teaching standard beginning courses in painting and drawing for five years.

Q Have you self-financed your business?

A The business is in the black, always. It always makes its way. I try not to borrow money, and I sometimes use a credit card, but I try to keep a real tight watch on it, and you have to or it gets away from you.

---

to new jobs, updating the costs of supplies and materials, and I add my labor, overhead and profit margin."—Carol Reed (see profile in chapter three)

You can budget both your operating expenses and capital expenses, that is, any fixed asset bought but not directly related to the cost of goods sold. The IRS publishes a schedule to help classify expenses as operating or capital. Capital expenditures may be amortized over the life of the equipment and accounted for in figuring your cost of doing business.

COST CONTAINMENT AND CONTROL

In the beginning you might have almost given your product away for any of a number of reasons:

- You were not in it for the money.
- It was a prototype used to work out the design uncertainties or to test the market or a new marketer.
- You were at the beginning of the learning curve in both product and pricing.

Assuming all that is behind you and you are making product and selling at a reasonable margin and volume, there are things you can look at to decrease costs and therefore increase profits or lower your product prices.

"One important point I make with students who want to get into this is that I only make a product line. I'm like Henry Ford . . . you can have any one of these chairs you want. The quickest way to lose your shirt in woodworking is to start making

things tailor-made to people's choices."—Michael Dunbar (see profile in chapter seven)

Materials

If you make your product in exotic hardwoods, forget about logging in South America or Thailand. But if you're into products of domestic woods, even as a hobbyist, you probably keep a keen eye out for a supply of burl or spalted woods from felled trees that are in somebody's way. Maybe your removing this wood will be sufficient payment to the owner and will furnish you with materials for many products.

You may work in materials not handled by the lumber supplier, so a little ingenuity and networking will be required to find suitable material.

Look for lumber dealers who wholesale to the trade. Usually a resale number will qualify you to make tax-exempt purchases and pass the sales tax on to the ultimate customer. (Or you may have to convince him that you are in the business and that your success will result in more business for the supplier.)

If you need large quantities of a single species, or even a mix, you can negotiate price, especially if you can set up a working relationship with the yard for future orders. They will be alerted to pointing out choice stock that, in their mind, would be a piece you would select.

Woodworker associations may have agreements with local merchants who cater to the woodworker, for discounted prices on materials and tools. The associations may also learn of a source and availability of large-quantity lots that could be purchased by a group of members. This can work the other way as well. If enough of you need some cherry or walnut, someone can find a good source at a good price for a sizable lot. And even if the quantity is not sizable enough to be delivered in a full truckload, shipping costs for LTL (less than a truckload) can be open to negotiation.

Making your expenses

Push quality to the max. There is a point in any process that extra effort beyond the proverbial 150 percent will not enhance the product in a proportional result. You can hand rub 100 coats of wax on a piece, but will it be ten times better, ten times more valuable because you exceeded the optimum finish of 10 applications? Perfectionists never achieve all that could be done, but there is a point where they have to say, "I'm finished."

Measure Your Marketing Costs

What is your return on investment (ROI) in advertising show participation and gallery promotions? You will have some history on the overall income and expenses, but some costs can be dissected, reduced to expense pools that can be evaluated on their merit and analyzed for their costs relative to their effectiveness. Is this a necessary, effective and affordable approach? This analysis is important when testing new programs, and also for reevaluating their continued need and associated costs down the road.

BUSINESS CYCLES

Is your product cyclical? Companies of all sizes are faced with managing outflow and income during business cycles.

Perhaps your product is spring/summer related, such as garden furniture or gardening tools, or you are a toy maker whose sales peak around the holidays. Maybe you create your own seasonal cycle, that is, you produce your wares in the off-season and hit the road or open shop in a seasonal resort.

National and global economies are based on economic cycles that may run counter to your planned business cycle. The customers may therefore postpone buying your product whose value and appeal was proved in better times.

Economic cycles may impact a sector of goods, such as new home sales—new homes that need your custom furniture and appointments—or buyers, who may have less discretionary funds available and change buying patterns, which could negativly impact sales. These cycles swing the other way at some point. Being ultraconservative may result in missing some opportunities during a down cycle.

Attracting new customers is as critical to the success of any business as knowing your financial position. They are the ones that keep the income flowing. Chapter seven covers topics including sales promotion, publicity, public relations, client search to bring in business, and pricing that will keep the customers coming.

Obviously your product must be exemplary, but this quality alone is not enough to promote growth. You must be (or hire) a marketer, for enthusiasm is contagious. Overcome any twinge of buyer remorse by building up the attributes, the special qualities and how fortunate the buyer is to have acquired such a treasure. Be humble, but proud of your work.

More Financial Tables

The statements in the following tables may have more detail than you currently need. Your future needs may call for a more complete, formal financial accounting approach to collect financial information to determine the status of the company and generate a picture of your profit direction. This level of reporting may be mandatory for obtaining financing and ultimately selling the business you have built.

Income statement, profit and loss statement and *operating statement* are all about the same thing: a summary of income and expenses for an accounting period (see page 94). The numbers, including the percent of sales for each item, will give you a clear picture of money coming in and going out. This is helpful when comparing activity with prior periods.

As an individual, you might want to figure your

	YEAR 1	YEAR 2	YEAR 3
Net Sales	_____	_____	_____
Cost to Produce	_____	_____	_____
Gross Margin	_____	_____	_____
Operating Expense	_____	_____	_____
Research, Development and Engineering	_____	_____	_____
Sales and Marketing	_____	_____	_____
General and Administrative	_____	_____	_____
Total Operating Income	_____	_____	_____
Interest Income	_____	_____	_____
Interest Expense	_____	_____	_____
Net Income (Loss) Before Taxes	_____	_____	_____
Taxes	_____	_____	_____
Net Income (Loss)	_____	_____	_____

Financial Projections

net worth, which is the present value of all your possessions—cash, investments, house, vehicles—minus outstanding debts, such as a mortgage, a revolving line of credit or notes due. If you do this at tax time each year, you can measure how you are doing financially. This exercise is recommended if you are managing both retirement and business needs.

See page 95 for a balance sheet for a business. (Owner's equity is known as *shareholders' equity* for a corporation.)

The balance sheet is the financial report that allows you to account for all assets and liabilities of the business, evaluate some key ratios within a reporting period and analyze changes and direction from year to year. This is also known as a statement of condition, showing the financial position on a particular date. This looks at the total assets compared with the liabilities.

Financial projections (see above table), regardless how crude, can be a target of where you are headed. If these projections fall short, or are exceeded, you find out why and adjust the projections based on more recent data.

	PERIOD	% OF TOTAL
Net Sales	_____	100.00%
Cost of Goods Sold		
Labor	_____	_____
Materials	_____	_____
Overhead	_____	_____
Delivery	_____	_____
Total	_____	
Gross Margin		
Selling Expense	_____	_____
General and Administrative	_____	_____
Total	_____	
Operating Profit	_____	_____
Interest	_____	_____
Profit Before Taxes	_____	_____
Income Taxes	_____	_____
Net Income (Loss)	_____	

Operating or Income Statement

	OPENING BALANCE	PERIOD 1	PERIOD 2
Assets:			
Cash	_____	_____	_____
Accounts Receivable	_____	_____	
Inventory	_____		
Fixed Assets	_____		
Accumulated Depreciation	_____		
Deferred Start-Up Costs	_____		
Total Assets	_____		
Liabilities:			
Accounts Payable			
Short-Term Debt			
Taxes Payable			
Long-Term Debt			
Total Liabilities			
Owner's Equity			
Total Liabilities and Owner's Equity			

Sample Balance Sheet

7

HOW DO I PRICE AND SELL MY WORK?

Study the conclusions reached in chapter six. Alter parameters to net your desired margins: reduce product cost, increase unit volume, increase price. Your skills are honed, the product is good, and you feel good about the product and about yourself.

PRICING YOUR WORK

Pricing your work to make money drives your search for the right marketplace, one that offers the best exposure and has format that will meet the price to produce your required net profit. Chapter one contains some thoughts on adjusting your costs and markets to find the right balance between value and price. This balance should be reevaluated periodically, especially when there is cause for review, which might be declining sales or unit profit margins, disappointing results of one of your products, or a product not doing well in a specific outlet. If you merchandise your work directly to the retail market, look at your own sales results. Any one of these could indicate the price is too high, either for the product's value or for where it is being marketed.

Conversely, a quick sellout, while nice, can indicate the price is set too low. Raise prices to where you still meet the sales goals, but maybe not quite so soon. Plow back any increase in price (and profit margins) into the business, for new development or just to use as a leveler for a future product or period that isn't quite as robust.

By now you may have read some of the secrets of successful pricing, as told by the profiled artisans, and you discovered that each has a different story. The key

here is that they do what works—for them. You will find your own secrets, fine-tuned by time and experience. The expected return of the part-timer just supplementing the coffers is different from the corporation meeting payroll, taxes, and every other cost in increased orders of magnitude.

Working from some target numbers is helpful to see where you are compared with where you want to be. Whether you meet those numbers from the beginning or during the first, fifth or tenth year, you have a basis for estimating your price and tracking the return on your investment in time, materials and the shop.

Price to the marketplace

Price is market driven and can go only as high as the competition and marketplace will permit. You, as the creative producer, bring together value—that is, design, execution, form and function—in whatever quantities needed to get you above the break-even point and into profit territory.

Enter the sample pricing exercise on page 100 from the target price side, assume that items comparable to yours are retailing for $100 in a gallery, and calculate how you can produce this item profitably at its wholesale price.

However, when approaching the pricing from a wishful labor rate, say $50 per hour instead of the $30 used in the example, the figures indicate you need to add a whole lot of value and look for an up-scale market that will support your price.

Can you find a gallery that can find a buyer who will shell out $265 for this item? Or do you have the

NAME: **Jonathan Simons, d/b/a Jonathan's Spoons**
LOCATION: **Kempton, Pennsylvania**
PRODUCT: **Cherry-wood spoons, holders, containers**
SINCE: **1978**
TRAINING: **B.A. Art/Design, University of Illinois**
SHOP: **Owns 1800-sq. ft. single-story building**
PRICING: **90 percent wholesale, 10 percent retail**
AFFILIATIONS: **National and regional ACC shows,**
    Philadelphia Market of American Craft Exhibitor.
    Advertises in Wendy Rosen's *NICHE* magazine and
    the ODCG's *Lifestyle Crafts*.

Jonathan Simons owns and operates Jonathan's Spoons. He mass markets his cherry-wood spoons through all the shows and galleries. Because he set his prices too low at his first national show, he experienced a first-hour sellout of his product.

Q **What event launched your change to full-time woodworking?**

A In Maine, in the winter, in the wake of the oil crisis and a huge drop in tourism, I was laid off from my job making caned seats for canoes. My garage workshop was not heated, so I bundled against the -20° temperature but couldn't glue parts for a wooden wheelbarrow I was making or the half-log stools, so I started cutting spoons.

Q **Who or what was most helpful?**

A In the initial phase of trying to make a living, it was probably a sales representative I worked with into the first year. Before that I was getting $30 to $35 orders, and he was bringing in $200 to $300 orders. He taught me how to wholesale.

Q **What was the most valuable skill or attribute you brought to the business?**

A I apprenticed with myself. When you apprentice, you get low wages but learn a lot. Maybe I was just frugal, but I paid myself a little and learned a lot, and it paid off.

Q **What obstacles did you encounter?**

A Probably a lack of capital—constantly fighting to save money for a new saw or a new bench. Ten years ago I couldn't even test a new band saw blade because if it didn't work out, it would be food off the table. Today, I can hop on an airplane and go see what I might want to add to the shop. And organization—just trying to stay ahead.

Q **What are your plans for growth?**

A I am almost where I want to be. I'm 80 percent there. I would like to grow another 20 percent, maybe in the next couple of years. I think I need to fill out my staff in marketing. I spend a lot of my time doing that, and more needs to be done in order to grow.

I read a book titled *The E-Myth*, by Michael Gerber, about small business and entrepreneurs.

His message was to get your business to a point that you can say, "There, I'm finished." He also suggested that you design your business as a franchising opportunity. If it's not worth selling, it's not worth owning.

Q How did you get started in the business?

A Well, my story is that I apprenticed with Jeffery Greene, a furniture designer in New Hope, Pennsylvania, for a short amount of time. One day while there, I forgot my spoon for the soup I brought, so I made one on the band saw. And a year later I was making them full-time. That was about 1978.

Q Where and how do you sell your work?

A Right now we are in about 1000 individual stores around the country and a few around the world. I don't use sales reps. I go to wholesale trade shows occasionally, and I advertise a little bit. I spend about ½ to 1 percent of my operating budget on advertising. I do *NICHE* magazine, which is Wendy Rosen's publication, and I do the ODCG's *Lifestyle Crafts*. I do about 10 percent retail at craft shows.

Q Of the 1000 outlets, do a few outproduce the others?

A Appalachian Springs, Simon Pearce Glass—successful client stores who are opening new stores seem to be the best. They already have experience with us and increase buying for their new stores. It gets to be a problem when they start opening close to the location of another successful store. So I have attempted a conflict policy. It's not exactly exclusive, but if somebody buys more than $500 of products a year, I make an effort to protect them. It's really impossible for me to enforce it, but at least the gesture is made.

Q Are you still going to shows, actively pursuing new outlets?

A Our target is to add about 20 percent a year, which is fairly rapid growth for me, but it's comfortable. That's probably what I've averaged since the beginning. And there is some attrition, but I don't have a percentage. And it's funny, you end up getting them back after a while. If they stay in business, five years later I'll get an account back that snubbed me before.

Q Of gift and craft shows to galleries, which is your prime target market?

A I meet the galleries through the gift shows, like the Rosen show; I'll meet new accounts. Maybe 10+ percent a year comes from word of mouth, or they saw the spoons somewhere. I call it the snowball effect. It seems that every year we grow, regardless of what I do. We've grown through recessions. One year I had 83 percent growth, and another year was 50 percent and another was 5 percent. The 80 and 50 percent growth is really hard to deal with. That means if you have three employees one year, the next year you have five. But the largest jump in employees was when I went from half an employee, a part-time guy, to a full-time person. That was the hardest jump. I have ten employees now in both the shop and office.

Q In the buyer's perception of what you produce, how do you rank quality, design, craftsmanship and price?

A I believe design is number one, and then price. Quality and craftsmanship seem to go together. The meaning of quality has changed over the years. Now I believe it means cheap. That's been the way it has been advertised.

Design, I mean original design, is the most important element. I've seen really creative original things not done real well but still sell if priced right.

Q What is your legal form of business?

A I became a corporation about two years ago, a C corporation, and I changed my fiscal year, and it has messed up all my thinking. I've got to let it run a few years and see if I get used to it.

Q Have you seen any advantage from incorporating?

A To my accountant. He gets to charge me twice a year. It kind of shifts income for half a year into the future. Other than that, you still have to pay the taxes. The C corporation seemed best because I keep having visions of grandeur, where I have multiple companies under one corporation, but I don't quite pull it together. And it's really a problem in the craft business because the whole industry has this mind-set against success, which grew from small roots. But there are a lot of decent-sized small businesses out there that are doing really good quality craft work, but it makes it difficult to get into some shows because they want the little guy there.

If today I set up my shop next to my shop 15 years ago, there would be no competition. I would sell ten times what he sells. I've spent the last 18 years figuring out which products are going to sell. This is an ongoing process.

Q What are your annual gross sales?

A Two years ago they were about $550,000, last year about $650,000 and this year they should be about $750,000. The year started slow, but it feels like we picked up in the last few months.

Q How long did it take you to get into the four-digit sales level?

A I started at $6,000, $9,000 my second, $11,000 my third year. I took quite a while to get up to the hundred thousands, probably seven or eight years.

Q Was there a major event that caused the jump?

A Hiring of full-time employees. I think I crossed over $100,000 with my second full-time employee. Hiring my first full-time employee is when I changed from more of a craft to more of a business—sort of a crossing line.

Q Are these all full-time employees? Any part-time?

A I have one part-time employee now, but part-time employees, for me, are very difficult to manage because they come and they go. When they come, they take up as much time as a full-time employee, and when they leave, you didn't get the work out of them. You just give them instructions to do something and they say, "Oh, I'm only going to be here for five more minutes." You might as well do the job yourself.

Q How did you finance your venture: self-financed, SBA loan?

A In the beginning I was self-financed. Later, I went to the bank, but it wasn't until I had a track record. That is such a hard thing to do to generate your own capital to work with. Somebody once suggested I get a small credit line and pay it off, whether I need it or not. And I learned early on to talk to the bank when I didn't need the money, and tell them when I would need the money. Then I would go back when I did need the money, and they would loan it to me. That worked very well. We didn't use the SBA route.

Generally I have a philosophy of borrowing about twice as much as I need. One of my greatest fears is to run out of cash. Two most important elements of running a business are profit and cash flow, and if you don't pay attention to both of them they can kill you . . . they can put you out of business. Some people only worry about cash flow until it's too late, and other people only worry about profit and don't cultivate the cash flow. By that I mean to go to the bank when you have money and ask for twice as much as you need, and borrow it and pay it back. If you borrow twice as much as you need, it's easy to pay it back.

Q **Was the financing part of an expansion?**

A With any growth—when you go to 80 percent growth in a year, which we have done—suddenly you have a need for capital. More tables, more ma-

chines. We were working out of a two-car garage and in a year we would need more space. I figured space would cost $200,000, and if we didn't buy, the interest avoided could be used toward adding a second story to the garage we were in. We got another three years out of the old property and had more equity in it when we moved.

PER UNIT		
Cost of materials	½ b.f. @ $3.00 a b.f.	$1.50
Labor		
Rough mill	.25 hours	
Cut and form	.75 hours	
Finish	.10 hours	
Shipping	.05 hours	
Total labor	1.15 hours @ $30 per hour	$34.50
Wholesale Price		$50.00
Gross Margin		$15.50
Gross Profit		31%

channels in place to retail it yourself at $133? If you have other work in galleries who mark up 40 and 50 percent, you really can't undercut price and still continue a good business relationship with the gallery owner or the customer who bought an item of lesser value but paid the markup. You really must decide which sales avenue is best for your products.

Labor and material costs

No set ratio exists for a piece's worth to the cost to produce it. The cost of material for one of Michael Dunbar's Windsor chairs represents 4 percent for his lowest-priced ($600) chair. Dean Douglas's willow

stick products include inexpensive natural woods, but are used effectively in his Southwestern style furnishings. And Michael Elkan prides himself on building a successful business based on using woods and wood forms that are unsuitable for much else.

If buying premium woods at premium prices, the product must also be premium. These costs need to be passed on. Rosewood or lignum vitae boxes will sell for more than ones made from pine or fir. Obviously the cost of material is greater, and so is your production time required to work harder, denser varieties of wood.

PER UNIT		
Cost of materials	½ b.f. @ $6.00 a b.f.	$3.00
Labor		
Rough mill	.25 hours	
Cut and form	1.50 hours	
Finish	.25 hours	
Shipping	.05 hours	
Total labor	2.05 hours @ $50 per hour	$102.50
Markup, G&A and Overhead at 30%		$30.75
Required price		$133.25

The point here is that you need to be realistic in your pricing expectations. Manage your time and your expenses in proportion to the value you produce. All units of all products will not net the same profit margin, but it is the accumulation of all you do that nets your return.

Know your costs

The how-much-to-charge exercise must begin somewhere, so begin with estimating the cost to produce, which may not have a direct bearing on what you charge. You have your own format for calculating this, but one example is shown on page 106.

Pricing programs can be set up in a spreadsheet with the labor rate and material costs plugged in. The program extends the estimated hours or units to cost per item or cost per production lot. A computer-based spreadsheet makes it easier to play what-if with the numbers.

On rare occasions, you might sell below your estimated price. At start-up it may be unintentional, or you might build a loss leader to get into a gallery. Another reason may be your dealings with the clients—maybe they're not affluent, but there are other valid reasons to take on the job.

"I do some pieces I probably should walk away from, knowing they can't really afford what the price should be, but it may be a new concept that can be worked on, so you take the job on and do it."—Mark Allen (see profile in chapter five)

PRESENTING YOUR WORK

Once again, what you sell and to whom will dictate the best sales approach.

Commissioned custom furniture and other pieces

If you do custom commissioned pieces, gather together a portfolio of your best photographs, news and feature articles, your biography and a list of references to present to gallery owners or prospective individual clients. Subtly ask the buyers of your past pieces to share their appreciation for your work with friends and associates. If you have a showroom in your shop or have your crafted furniture and accessories in your home, invite prospects to come and see what you do.

NAME: **Michael Dunbar**

LOCATION: **Hampton, New Hampshire**

PRODUCT: **Windsor Chairs (production and instruction)**

SINCE: **1970**

TRAINING: **Self-taught**

SHOP: **New 2400 sq. ft. two-story facility on property with the family homestead**

PRICING: **Retail only**

AFFILIATIONS: **Conducts seminars on Windsor chair making. Author of *Make a Windsor Chair With Michael Dunbar*, Taunton Press, 1984.**

Michael Dunbar prices his Windsor chairs based on their value, not the cost to produce. He augments income with his week-long chair building classes. Recently he moved into new facilities on his property in New Hampshire.

Q What event launched your woodworking career?

A A hobby that got out of hand.

Q What obstacles did you encounter?

A No place to work, and never really having enough money, always making do. And, people were another obstacle; in the early years, acquaintances were not 100 percent supportive. Self-confidence is valuable; you have to believe in yourself. The thing about supportive people is when you're down, they're up, and vice versa. A wife's (or husband's) support is invaluable. If the spouse is not supportive, the venture is doomed to fail.

Q What are your plans for growth?

A I'm now 50 years old. Fifteen more years at the bench and I won't be able to teach anymore. It is really a draining experience. I might think about expanding my quarterly newsletter into a periodical, as editor and publisher.

Q How did you begin?

A I had no interest in being a woodworker. I was in college, planning to get my doctorate in French and teach at the university level, when I bought a Windsor chair at a yard sale—an antique Windsor—and was very much captivated by the chair. I went out to find out what this thing was. From a book in the local library I discovered I had this antique Windsor. It occurred to me that if having one antique Windsor was such a pleasant experience, I wanted to own more. At antique shops I discovered that what I bought was a real accident. Even then, Windsors were $200+; they're now in the multi-thousand range. So I bought broken ones and fixed them, and I taught myself woodworking that way. I finally reached a point that I could fix anything on a Windsor, and figured I must be good enough to tackle a whole chair, so I did.

Still trying to learn more about these chairs, I went to museums and antique shops asking a lot of questions, and they asked why I was asking. I told them that I was making these chairs and they asked if I would bring some in to see. I fell into a market that I didn't know existed, making a product that I had never intended to make.

Q Were you a student at this time?

A By the time I graduated with a bachelor's degree I was making chairs for a living. I couldn't go to graduation because I had an order for 25 chairs.

Q Who showcases your work?

A I won't deal with any middlemen. I deal directly with customers. I always have. It's too hard making a living giving 40 percent of something to someone who has a storefront. There are plenty of people out there who will buy directly from me. The problem is getting them to know that I'm making chairs. In my case, I understand publicity, public relations and the power of media.

I don't have to go through middle-people; I'm able to do it myself. I would recommend this to anybody because that extra 40 percent off of what you're making is a tremendous amount of profit. You're in a really competitive environment if you are a chair maker and you're making chairs and putting them in a gallery at 40 percent off. I'm a chair maker, and I don't have to put them in a gallery. I can sell directly to the public. I'm making a heck of a lot more money, and I can lower my prices and squeeze you out.

Woodworking has become intensely competitive, and anybody who has to be selling through a gallery instead of selling directly to the public is at a very strong disadvantage.

Q How do you get the word out?

A I do press releases, and the press release is a decent way to get the media to pay attention. The problem with a press release—and I can tell you this as an editor—is a ton of these come across their desks and most of them go right in the circular file. A few may be filed for future reference, and every now and then, one will draw a response right off the bat.

In my case what I was doing was novel enough to attract the news media and attract public attention. One thing I did was respond to an ad in *Early American Life* magazine, published by The Early American Society, and they asked about making Early American crafts for them. I sent some photographs and got an order for a chair and a query about how much it would cost to make 25. So I stumbled right onto a marketplace. *Early American Life* bought 25 chairs and ran a full-page ad in their magazine to advertise my chairs to the public. I quickly became well known to a marketplace that sustained me for a long time.

What I recommend when people taking my classes ask how to get started, is to go home and get your neighbor, your sister-in-law, or somebody to call the local newspaper and say, "I've just stumbled on to the most incredible thing. There's a guy over here on Elm Street who's making chairs from logs. He gets these logs, he splits them up and is making these incredibly beautiful chairs. I just thought you guys ought to know about it."

And then what happens, in the mind of a reporter (this is much better than a press release): This is an eyewitness who saw this, and this is a third party. This is a very important concept in marketing—a third-party endorsement. You can advertise until you're blue in the face. You can say how wonderful your chairs are, but it's you talking. Somebody else says how wonderful your chairs are and they listen.

So the reporter is more likely to call you and say, "I just got a phone call from somebody who says you make these chairs from logs." Now you have a reporter on the hook and you get your first story written about yourself. That's the most important one you'll ever get, because news media all read each other, and they feel if it is in print in some other magazine that it's valid.

The odds are pretty good that you'll get a second call. The incredible thing about publicity is the more you get, the more you're going to get. It's like a rock rolling down a hill—it picks up speed.

And that's relatively inexpensive as an

approach. You're not buying ads. And it's all third-party validated.

When I do an interview, and I still do an awful lot of them with newspapers, I specifically ask that they put in these two facts:

The first thing is my chairs start at $600 apiece. What that's going to do is rule out the people who are thinking, *Gee, we need a new set of kitchen chairs. Let's go down to JCPenney. I read this article about this guy who makes chairs down on Elm Street. Let's go see him first.* They're thinking $79 per chair, and they walk in and yours are $600 a chair. The first thing they do is blanch, then they say something that's probably going to hurt your feelings. They feel bad about you; you feel worse about yourself. So I have them put in the price to weed out the tire kickers.

The second thing I ask they put in is that I don't fix chairs. As soon as there's a newspaper or magazine article, I get calls from little old ladies who want me to fix a kitchen chair or a chair that's up in the attic, or someone is looking for bar stools.

Q How would you rank the importance of quality, design, craftsmanship and delivery?

A The standard pitch that I give to my students when they are starting a project: You always have four objectives in mind when you make a piece of furniture. First, it has to perform its function. If it's a chair, you've got to be able to sit in it; a table, you have to be able to sit at it; and you have to be able to sleep on a bed. The second is related to the first, in that it has to be comfortable. You can sit on rock; it doesn't make it a chair. It has to be comfortable after you sit in it for a long time. The third is you have to produce something with enough quality to endure. It has to be strong. It has to live up to people's expectations. And the fourth, which is the one I think separates masters from journeymen: It has

to be good-looking. It has to be designed well enough so that people stop and appreciate it.

Q How many varieties or variations of the Windsor do you make?

A I make a Windsor Sack Back, a Continuous Arm, a High Back, a Fan Back, Oval Back and a Writing Arm chair. One important point I make with students who want to get into this is that I only make a product line. I'm like Henry Ford . . . you can have any one of these chairs you want. I don't make changes or alterations. The quickest way to lose your shirt in woodworking is to start making things tailor-made to people's choices.

First, you can never recover all the time that goes into new jigs, calculations, setup, then discovering it doesn't work, and having to do it over again. That is lost time that you'll never get back. You couldn't raise your price enough to get it back. The second reason is you are going to end up making things that you don't particularly like because you have let somebody who may not know what they are talking about dictate your decisions.

Probably the most important defense, the things that will get you through being self-employed, are your self-respect, your self-esteem, your self-confidence. If those aren't there, you're likely to wash out.

Q What is your legal form of business?

A Sole proprietor. My accountant and lawyer say it is not worth the paperwork to incorporate. I don't have the corporate veil, but I don't have employees or anything from which I can be removed. Anything that is done, I'm the one who did it. They said the best thing I could do was have a good insurance policy, so that's what I carry. I have a business policy. It covers me for liability, for casualty, for fire and theft. It covers product liability plus liability for my business.

Q Without divulging how much you're making, what is your year-to-year increase over time to where you are now?

A Last year, I came very close to grossing $100,000. And I should meet it this year. The new facility will improve things greatly. One problem in my last shop was I didn't live nearby, and the office was at the house. And if I spent five hours in the office paying bills, then I wasn't going to the shop across town for three hours. Now I'm living here on the same property, and I go into the shop whenever I need to. I go to the shop every day because the office is up here. If I need to do any work, I go downstairs. I'm much more productive that way.

The shop also has allowed me to do a number of other things that I wasn't able to do in the past. I now have storage for wood, so I can buy wood in1000-board foot lots and I can buy at the mill and I can air-dry it, so I can buy at $1 a board foot instead of $3.60. And although I have more up-front investment, I reap the savings over the long haul.

Q What about your financing?

A All self-financed. I do have a line of credit set up but haven't used it yet. A couple of things are coming up. We are forming an association with John and Joyce Nelson to hold scroll saw classes. "Scroll Saw Central" will use the facilities for maybe ten weekend classes. The Windsor chair classes are now up to 23 weekends. The other times the training facility is idle, so I thought this might be a good way to expand the use of the facility to offset the cost of the building.

I wrote a book for American Country Woodworkers where the editor wanted one chapter on amortizing the cost of everything prorated into one item. I don't look at it that way. A building is expensive to own and operate, with taxes, electric and water bills and upkeep. I haven't figured how the cost of the facility relates to each chair. I look at it as if I sell several chairs per week, I will meet expenses.

Mail a primo shot of your work to newspapers and magazines in hopes that one or two will find it interesting enough to print, or to report on your activities, as described by Jon Sauer and Michael Dunbar. Prepare a brochure, a catalog, or just a flyer of your newest piece and mail to galleries, or as a piece sent out to answer an Internet inquiry, taking Sal Maccarone's approach.

Exhibiting at shows

Acceptance at any show, whether it is a local showcase of an association's work or a more commercial venue for generating direct sales, can be an indicator of a broader appreciation for the product.

However, this is no assurance that it's a good test because there may be economic factors at work in your community that impact sales volumes and prices you might expect in a more affluent area, especially if selling high-end items. And too, you may be known as the offspring of a handyman or cabinetmaker, but you want to make and sell a $2000 table, where your father might have produced something as functional (but not as beautiful, but don't tell him that) for far less.

"A fellow came up to our booth at one craft show and said, 'I wouldn't sell this piece for less than $75.' The point was we weren't selling it for $40; why would we want to not sell it for $75?"—David Lomas/Debra Doucette (see profile in chapter one)

Whether wholesaling or retailing your work, get your product in front of buyers at local, regional or national shows. Some smaller shows are organized to promote interest in local artisans/woodworkers by

MAN HOURS (MH)	RATE	PRICE
Labor @ $30 per hour		
Rough milling	0.1 hour	
Cutting and shaping	0.5 hour	
Assembling	0.2 hour	
Finish sanding	0.1 hour	
Finishing	0.05 hour	
Total labor	0.95 × $30	$28.50
Materials*	0.5 bf @ $3.25	$1.63
Total unit cost		$30.13
Target sale price		$50.00
Gross profit		$19.87
Gross Margin		40%

*This could be a comprehensive bill of materials if the project is complex.

Cost Estimate Calculator

showcasing members' work. Other shows are more profit driven, catering to both retail customers and wholesale buyers, gallery owners, or buyers for mail-order catalogs or corporate premiums. At some of the major shows, certain times may be set aside for whole-salers only, to discuss your product, pricing and delivery commitments. Other times the show is open for the retail public.

Find and test the marketplace that has the most promising buyer base, or tailor your product to a marketplace you want to enter. The product could be a lower-end item that could be used to fill the production schedule during your formative years and beyond. Building income producers to meet your interim goals not only helps to keep a positive cash flow, but also broadens your client base and opens the possibility of future, higher-end business referrals. Don't ignore the business potential of anyone who shows an interest in what you produce. Analyze your target market; set

your sights toward a gallery or show that has the best potential of promoting your product to the right prospective buyer.

Finding shows, exhibits and fairs

Set your sights on an upcoming street fair, arts/craft show, county or state fair or a nearby arts/craft festival or exhibition. Wood and woodworking suppliers in your area should have information, and maybe entry forms, to local events.

As a member of the woodworking community, keep abreast of what's happening in your surrounding area. Find out what shows are coming up and how successful other local artisans/woodworkers have been in selling their wares. If the product-buyer match is a good fit for what you make, you can do some business and make your presence known. Even if you feel the match isn't right on, do one or two shows just for the experience if you haven't shown your work before.

Maybe it is your local woodworker association's annual show. You can be a spectator and observe activity on a local level, or you can pitch in as a volunteer and get closer to the thoughts behind the work and to the public's reactions. Better still, submit an entry or two of your work, preferably representative of what you want to bring to market, just for the exposure. Volunteer to work even if you enter. Getting involved helps the networking effort.

If you are past that local phase, branch out to larger shows to test a broader market segment, or do a more specialized show to test a specific buying segment. Keep searching for a better fit for what you make. Major shows may be general, exhibiting crafts in all mediums. You may find smaller shows aimed at specific buyer interests in types (such as furniture, gifts, toys, culinary wares) or styles (Shaker, Victorian, Arts and Crafts, and so forth).

Magazines are a great resource and time-saver. Woodworker magazines, both regional and national, contain schedules of events, articles, and maybe a call for entries to upcoming shows. Magazines and newsletters are quick, concise sources of information for the woodworker looking for new venues to visit. Many report on upcoming shows, symposia and workshops by date and location.

Ron Goldman's *Woodworker West*, Los Angeles, does a fine job of listing West Coast events and reports on the event results. *Woodwork*, published in Novato, California, contains "Events of Interest to Woodworkers." *Woodshop News*, out of Essex, Connecticut, covers custom woodworking from a business and recreational angle. *Popular Woodworking*, Cincinnati, Ohio, publishes a calendar of events of interest. *American Woodworker* and *Fine Woodworking* contain similar information, and the list goes on. These pages help you plan your strategy for the shows and events on the horizon.

Magazines from major promoters of craft shows deal more with their particular events. *American Craft* is the magazine of the American Craft Council. The Rosen Group publishes *NICHE* magazine for retailers of American craft, *AmericanStyle* magazine for collec-

tors of fine American craft and *Crafting as a Business* for artisans and craftspeople in the business.

If you want to research events farther out or find out what's happening in a particular show or market, your library may have a copy of the *Directory of North American Fairs, Festivals, & Expositions*. This is published annually, as is *A Guide to World Fairs/Festivals 1997*. These offer a good rundown of the major scheduled events for the year.

While you are in the library, another reference source is the *Encyclopedia of Associations*, which lists 30,000 organizations, a few of which may be of interest to the producing woodworker. This multivolume set lists trade associations to shows and exhibits. As you become known, many of these promoters will find you.

Promoters and sponsors of shows and exhibitions

To broaden your approach, attend some of the American Crafts Council shows, or a Rosen Gift show, or similar events that showcase American craftspeople. Investigate any show you might want to try, if just to check out what is being done and the organizer's presentation. Talk to exhibitors for any insight and any tips they will share.

AMERICAN CRAFT COUNCIL

American Craft Council/American Craft Enterprises conducts six major fairs a year throughout the U.S. Their draw is impressive, and those fortunate enough to make it in are usually pleased with the results. That is not to say other shows won't do as well for you. When and if you get into these shows (see chapter eight, for information on entry requirements and committee selection) be prepared to produce and deliver in quantity.

THE ROSEN GROUP

Their semiannual "Buyer's Market of American Craft," held in Philadelphia, Pennsylvania, showcases more than 2500 artisans to galleries and craft retailers. The Rosen shows are just one part of this craft support organization. Chapter eight contains more information on how you can be taken under the wing of this promoter, who provides other marketing opportunities to help artists achieve success.

THE WOODWORKING SHOWS

This is a group that organizes more than a dozen regional shows nationwide that primarily exhibit manufacturers of woodworking tools, supplies and resources. They also have regionally and nationally acclaimed woodworkers offering demonstrations and workshops. Call their main office in Los Angeles at (800) 826-8257 for information about shows near you.

What to bring to a show

Shows have different guidelines for what you can and cannot do to the space you rent. Some show organizers adhere to a strict code for signage, tables and cases, while others allow the exhibitors some freedom of presentation. You will probably be asked to personally man your booth and not substitute an associate during a set number of hours. When you're not there, place a guest log for interested buyers or admirers to jot down their kudos and maybe an address for follow-up. Show organizers hire security personnel for after-hours surveillance, but consider the protection of locked cases for small items, and maybe string a rope across furniture to prevent someone from taking a snooze on your $5000 bench with his feet propped up on the $2500 occasional table.

Jon Sauer, with his intricate ornamental turnings, goes to shows prepared. The most recent addition to his show kit is a zippered vinyl booth cover that can be closed after hours. Products are locked away in Plexiglas cases and pyramids and are hidden from view as well.

Requirements for selection are outlined in chapter eight. Delivery and fulfillment quotas or commitments are part of the selection agreement, and the obligation is on the exhibitor to fill orders as requested. There is some leeway here, but the promoter wants to keep the buyer happy and coming back for more. Promoters want to be assured that the designer-producer can meet delivery, as well as quality, commitments.

Also bring a positive attitude and a little bit of the theatrical. Get your mind-set aligned to the format. If showing at a street fair, be ready for all comers. You don't need to be a barker or a clown, but don't be an ultraserious businessperson either. This format is an invitation for bargaining and bartering—a game you don't want to play, but don't get perturbed. You're next to the tarot card reader, just up from the shrunken heads, so don't take yourself too seriously. If at a Renaissance fair, be ready to joust with the jesters and gnaw on barbecued ribs; see what interest you can coax out of the merrymakers.

At an art colony festival, don't wear the suit and tie (if you have them). Be focused but be loose. And at the national wholesale show, be the capable designer/producer who can provide value and quantity to meet the buyer's needs, today and beyond.

Think of how the customer wants to perceive the artisan. Act yourself, but adapt to the setting as well.

AT THE POINT-OF-SALE DISPLAY

- Plan the space to attract interested buyers. Randy Bader takes the time to build complementing pieces to show a vignette of his work in an attractive combination and setting.
- Be present; be open; be the host or hostess. Place yourself where you can acknowledge visitors without appearing to attack them on approach or to corner them with a pitch.
- Lighting, signage, tables, cases and placement of larger pieces should create an inviting atmosphere.
- Have a stand for the guest log, your business cards, a portfolio of your work, your biography and press clippings handy for visitors' perusal.

DEALERS AND GALLERIES

Area co-ops and associations, whether or not they are local to where you live and produce, can be helpful in showcasing and selling your work. Some may be operating under a charter that limits the area they draw from or the types of styles they represent, but there is one or more out there for what you produce. Some galleries sell to walk-in trade and publish catalogs of the craftspeople's work.

Theme or style retailers may be right for you whether you are producing modern, Arts and Crafts, Stickley, Craftsman Country, Southwestern, Appalachian or Shaker. If you produce gallery type items, find the gallery or galleries that cater to your targeted buyers. You can find them by targeting an area and a gallery you feel can sell your work at your price. Local galleries are a good place to start, and to stay if the fit between what you make and what they sell is right. Buyers are interested in buying locally crafted goods, especially in geographical pockets known for their heritage of styles or history.

The Southwestern, the Shaker, the Adirondacks, the prairie, and the old-world styles of the Northeast draw such interest. Visitors appreciate these roots and these pools of talent and skill. Seaports always draw visitors and locals alike in search of nautical-themed wood and art crafts.

Without ranking the galleries that cater to fine woodworking and truly represent fine artisans, there may be a hierarchy in the products they handle, but there is no pinnacle, no one Utopia that is best (an opinion not shared by the gallery management). Each of the thousands of retail galleries caters to a target market comprising different tastes, different needs and drawing different clientele.

> "I really appreciate the screening done by the gallery staff. It saves me a lot of wasted breath. I want the customer to know what they're coming for and be ready to buy at my price."—Jennifer Schwarz (see profile in chapter four)

Finding the right match for what you make is important to your success if you intend to market through a representative gallery. It doesn't have to be the most elite, just the most effective in achieving sales results for your items.

Regional guilds and their galleries

Associations, co-ops and guilds have found success in representing their members in their organizations' re-tail ventures. Local associations may have residency or membership requirements. Other galleries, independently owned or operated by a guild, association or co-operative, are open to members and may invite outside producers.

OHIO DESIGNER CRAFTSMEN GUILD

One such organization is the Ohio Designer Craftsman Guild (ODCG) which, from its Ohio Crafts Museum in Columbus, has a number of marketing operations:

- Operates retail studios in Ohio under the name A Show of Hands, selling products by Ohio designer artisans.
- Publishes *Lifestyle Crafts*, a semiannual catalog of craftspeople and their work. The catalog generates 17,000 inquiries per issue.
- Distributes Lifestyle Crafts to 20,000 retailers semiannually.
- Produces and presents the Ohio Designer Craftsmen Fairs in Cleveland, Indianapolis, Cincinnati and Columbus.
- Represents guild members at major shows, distributing *Lifestyle Crafts* and coordinating buyer inquiries.

NORTHWEST GALLERY OF FINE WOODWORKING, SEATTLE, WASHINGTON

The Northwest Gallery of Fine Woodworking is an association of woodworkers, but craftspeople need not be members to have their work accepted. The commission rate, however, depends on member status. Christopher Brooks, Director, a marketer par excellence, recently relocated the main gallery from a smaller space into a nearby, newly refurbished corner showroom in the Pioneer Square District of Seattle.

A gallery branch, located in nearby Kirkland, caters to slightly different clientele. To promote the gallery and the artisans showcased there, special events are heavily advertised to draw in and educate the public on finer handcrafted ware. Recently a chair show was assembled, where customers could see the artistry of Stickley, Nakashima, Maloof, etc., intermixed with

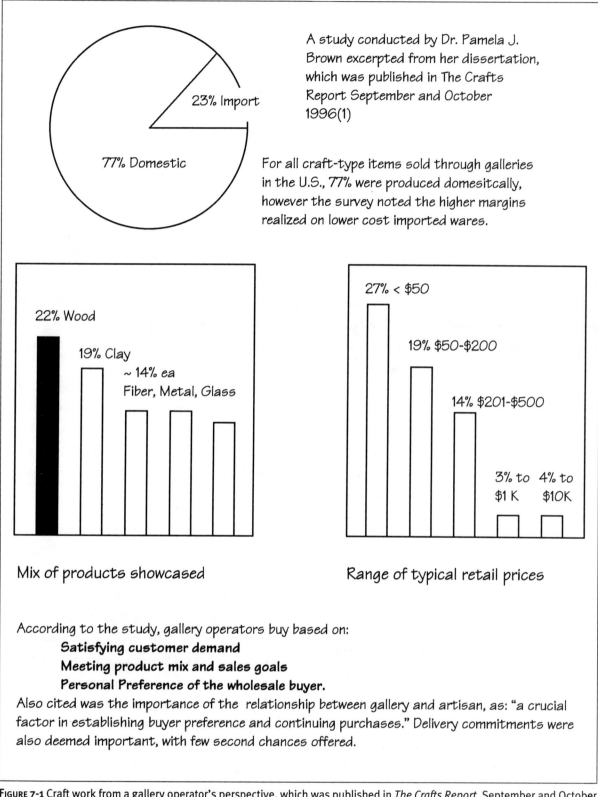

A study conducted by Dr. Pamela J. Brown excerpted from her dissertation, which was published in The Crafts Report September and October 1996(1)

For all craft-type items sold through galleries in the U.S., 77% were produced domesitcally, however the survey noted the higher margins realized on lower cost imported wares.

23% Import

77% Domestic

22% Wood

19% Clay

~ 14% ea
Fiber, Metal, Glass

Mix of products showcased

27% < $50

19% $50-$200

14% $201-$500

3% to
$1 K

4% to
$10K

Range of typical retail prices

According to the study, gallery operators buy based on:

Satisfying customer demand

Meeting product mix and sales goals

Personal Preference of the wholesale buyer.

Also cited was the importance of the relationship between gallery and artisan, as: "a crucial factor in establishing buyer preference and continuing purchases." Delivery commitments were also deemed important, with few second chances offered.

FIGURE 7-1 Craft work from a gallery operator's perspective, which was published in *The Crafts Report*, September and October 1996. Reprinted with permission.

what is being done today. Again, marketing is a process, not an event.

Commercial galleries

In addition to the above outlets, many other outlets are available to the artisan. Galleries create product mixes based on mediums, fine and functional art, period (mixed or pure), style or purpose.

SAWBRIDGE STUDIOS, CHICAGO

Sawbridge Studios in the Chicago area is the brainchild of Paul Zurowski and his two partners, all of whom come from the marketing side of corporate America.

They accept biographies of craftspeople and slides of their work. After four years, they continue to grow but haven't looked too far west of the Mississippi, although they plan to expand their artisan base. Their two studios feature a variety of handcrafted pieces, primarily in wood, but also in crystal, ceramic and some iron work. Much of what they showcase is traditional or renditions based on the traditional. Cited was some work from Marshall Petty, 18th-century reproductions—Queen Anne and Chippendale style furniture. Charles Shackleton's furniture produced in the old-world style is among the favorites there (see profile in chapter one), and Sawbridge has helped develop a line of prairie furniture produced by Steve Stenger and Ron Skidmore. This line was cocreated through Sawbridge's vision of a need and the woodworker's interpretation of how to design a whole line to go with a chair.

Sawbridge Studios, like other studios, merchandises their individual craftspeople. They create a gallery atmosphere, focus attention on the artist with a bio board, include their work in their database and catalog and have information for interested buyers who may be in the market for a commissioned piece, or a piece modified to suit individual tastes.

OTHER GALLERIES

The Real Mother Goose in Portland, Oregon, Appalachian Spring in Washington, DC, del Mano Gallery, Los Angeles (Brentwood) California, and the Craftsman Guild in San Francisco, California, are among those mentioned by the profiled group. These and others provide the craftsperson with the opportunity to show and to sell. A trip through the local telephone directory might provide some leads for further consideration.

Art shows

There are pockets of creativity throughout the country, and some forward-thinking, enterprising individual may have seen the potential and organized a show, festival or similar event. A few of the shows used by the profiled artisans include:

Laguna Festival of the Arts, Laguna Beach, California, hosted by an established art community each summer. The **Sawdust Festival** runs concurrently just up the road in Laguna Beach.

San Diego County's Del Mar Fair houses the annual **Design in Wood** show. Check your local listings for comparable outlets in your area.

AN AFFLUENT AREA CAN'T HURT

The Festival of the Arts, held each year in Laguna Beach, California, is a juried show of area artists and craftspeople. The call for entries brings in more than three hundred replies. All entrants are from the same economic area and share a higher production cost overhead, which makes prices comparable. Many use this as their one show a year and many derive their livelihood from this one source.

Artisans from other areas also rely on one show (or two) to bring in work for the following year.

HOW DO I GROW MY BUSINESS?

You planned, you built and finally reached your business objectives, whether motivated by profit, your creative drive or just another challenge to be faced and conquered. You need to know when you've arrived and decide whether or not to stretch to the next plateau.

REVIEW/RENEW YOUR INTERESTS AND DIRECTION

Does the business remain craft driven, or somewhere along the way did it become more profit motivated? There is nothing wrong with either one, if it meets the current and future objectives.

Working with your hands, producing something of lasting beauty may have been the impetus for the woodworking venture, and it may be important to you to keep the original values—the spark—alive in your business. Perhaps you're spending less time woodworking and more time selling, or you don't want to grow away from your hands-on work to become the successful administrator, manager or overseer of a larger business. Determine what path and level of growth your business should take.

Stay put

Some of the profiled artisans have been there, have done that, and have retrenched to a comfortable operating level. There is a belief that it's hard to stay in the middle and make a go of it, meaning that unless you continue to grow, failure is more likely. That may be true for many businesses, but handcrafted value can sustain a person in the middle ground, especially where that person can weave a mystique, an aura, a value surrounding the work he or she produces that sell both the artisan and her work.

Grow Larger

Some believe handcrafted creations of an individual artisan may be held in higher esteem than those crafted by 5 or 10 or 30 individual artisans employed in a company. But this grouping and pooling of talent and resources allows certain economies not available to the sole producer and therefore may permit more competitive pricing in the marketplace. Being employees/artisans doesn't alter the fact that they too can perpetuate the craft by producing quality goods. Eager employees can absorb, learn and launch a more personal endeavor, if that's their goal, after having served a full-wage apprenticeship with a larger company.

Whether you decide to stay where you are or to grow is your choice. But even when staying put, growth in product and client base is required to maintain your comfortable level. Regardless of whether you choose to stay a producing artisan or operate a larger business, there are some aspects common to both that should be revisited to at least sustain your business.

You've done something right

In order to get to this point in your business you've probably done many things right. You now have the advantage of knowing which accomplishments can be built on and which events were not accomplishments after all, but something to be written off to experience.

Growth of a business is relative; it depends on

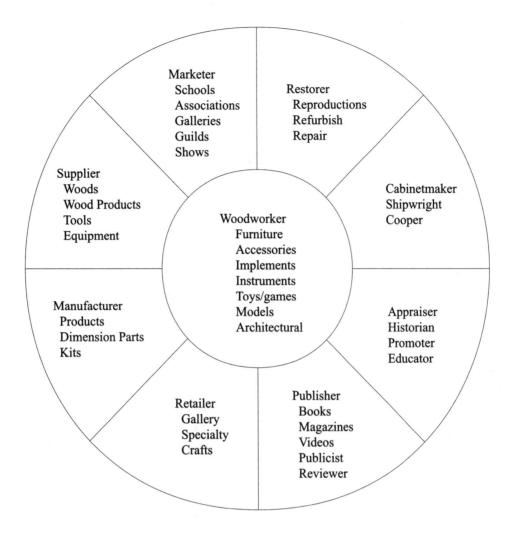

FIGURE 8-1 Derivatives

your starting point. The building process started at the beginning, and the steps and leaps you took along the way were proportional to the business size. Hiring a second employee can have the same impact that a larger company experiences when they double their staff from 10 to 20 employees.

Formalize your business plan

Update your business plan—your initial answers to, when? where? why? etc.—into a more definitive plan that spells out how you built a profitable business and how you intend to grow that business.

As the business grows more complex, you need to better define where the company is headed. This more formal plan can be used to entice lenders and backers if outside financing is to be part of the growth package.

The business plan should detail where you were, where you are and where you are headed. Future financial backers—or someone interested in buying your business—will want to see a plan.

Your plan can be formatted as individual pages, to be updated as the business develops along the planned route, as follows:

1. Business objectives
   - Reasons for starting and operating your venture
   - The niche, need and function it fills

- The new niche, need, function it will fill in the future

2. Business form
   - Legal form of business
   - Organization
   - Licenses, permits

3. Resumes of yourself and other key persons
   - What you bring to the business
   - What they bring to the business

4. Product and product mix
   - What you produce

5. Production plan
   - How you produce it

6. Materials
   - Supplies
   - Supplier agreements

7. Production facilities
   - What you need to produce it

8. Equipment
   - Inventory
   - Planned purchases

9. Marketing plan
   - How you sell it

10. Major outlets, clients
    - Who you sell to or through
    - How you sell; percentage of wholesale, retail, consignment

11. Competition
    - Others doing similar things
    - Why you're better; your edge

12. Financials
    - Past and current results
      Operating statements
      Balance sheets
    - Forecast of future results
      Financial projections

13. Copies of past business tax returns

14. Business references
    - Bank
    - Suppliers
    - Personal

Where to look for growth

If you need to increase production, what additional resources might be required? Can these costs be recouped in the added sales volume?

Would your product and operational objectives allow a move up the production ladder from:
- one-of-a-kind custom
- limited production custom
- production, semicustom
- mass production

Finding new business, new customers

Every business, regardless of size and age, needs new clients. When you sell directly to the ultimate user, your well-built, long-lasting product will not need replacing for a generation or so. However, that client may buy, and encourage his circle of friends to buy, other furniture or accessories if he appreciates and enjoys your work. And you must seek out new customers, end users and wholesalers alike, to keep the flow going. Attrition can erode your client base. New outlets not only become the lifeblood of growth but sustain your business as well.

Widen your promotional reach:
- advertise
- direct mail
- shows and festivals (local, regional, national)

When doing it all, as in self-promotion, step into this list at whatever point you need to expand your story.
- A business card or capabilities blurb in the local woodworker's place of business.
- Classified ad in the local decorator/home magazine.
- A small display ad in the local decorator/home magazine.
- Advertise in major newspapers, magazines.

	ONE-OF-A-KIND	LIMITED PRODUCTION	SEMICUSTOM	PRODUCTION
Current				
Product	Chair A	Toy A		
Units/year	10 at $800 each	50 at $40 each		
% Capacity				
Labor	50%	20%		
Shop	50%	10%		
Sales	$8000	$2000		
% Sales	80%	20%		
Expanded				
Product			Chair A	Toy A
Units/year			30 at $800 each	100 at $40 each
% Capacity				
Labor			50%	20%
Shop			50%	10%
Sales			$24,000	$4000
% Sales			80%	20%

Production Modes

- Advertise in newspapers and magazines with national coverage.
- Advertise in gallery buyers' publications, such as The Rosen Group's *NICHE* magazine, or the ODCG's *Lifestyle Crafts*. Special-interest publications reaching followers of trends, movements and styles might be right for your product.

Responses to these inquiries can be a brochure, a flyer or a card, but follow up with a telephone call to see how you might be of assistance. Also consider organizing these prospects in some kind of database file.

Building a database

A client list builds with each inquiry, contact or sale. You may have a guest book or a stack of reply cards placed conveniently next to your display booth for collecting comments, names and (hopefully) addresses. With some sleuthing, you can get an address for use in mailing show announcements, a new product introduction or periodic reminders that you're still producing.

This information can be simply compiled on ledger cards, on handwritten lists, or on pieces of paper thrown into a drawer. A handwritten or typed list is a database. A computer is useful for entering data and extracting selected data sorted almost any way you like it. But how helpful it will be is determined by how you structure the information.

Look at the different types of information that may have future value to your business. A database that includes client names, addresses and telephone numbers can be structured to create labels or calling lists for prospects who have expressed an interest in a selected item or line. It can produce a list of attendees to a past annual show. You can extract and format these data in personalized notes or letters (without the impersonal "Dear First Middle Last Name" approach).

In the same record, or another database linked to the master list, you can include other fields of personal information, such as past inquiries, past purchases, personal preferences, purchasing power, types of items, birth dates and anniversary dates to be used in promotion along with the more generalized holidays (Christmas or Hanukkah, Valentine's Day, Mother's Day, etc). Begin with a plan of what type of information you may need.

- Sales contact (name of customer, gallery buyer)
- Business name
- Address
- City
- State
- Zip code
- Telephone
- Fax
- Referred by (add name here and above as sales contact)
- Event (which show, ad, sales call)
- Item
- Terms

- Date

All you want to do is collect different types of data, linked by keywords. All related information about a person or a job number is linked as a record.

As the database grows, you can pull out information related to an individual item, purchaser, payment terms, date. You can bring up reports on who inquired about a particular item, how many customers you have in a zip code area, how many referrals by an individual, how many referrals from a particular item, etc.

If your business requires a bit more organization, and the volume of names has grown substantially, a computer can be handy in recording and sorting this information for future use. Computers can crunch a lot of data—to track complex transactions and a kaleidoscope of information in each record and to link records under certain parameters.

Spreadsheet and database programs included with many home/office software packages, such as Microsoft Works or Corel's WordPerfect, are more than adequate to organize your records. A spreadsheet is a fixed format, changeable but not too flexible, but works in a pinch, or if your needs are fairly simple. Database information can be reformatted to suit the query.

A record can be a string of fields associated with a person or business (client or prospect), a product, an expense or whatever like information you assign to each column of fields. A database can be changed to suit your future needs, but it is easier if you start off right. You can query the database by one or more of the fields and keywords within a field to build a report based on what information you want to extract.

Build on past accounts and network contacts

From the database, pull out all your gallery contacts and conduct a survey. Find out what each gallery owner's plans are for the future. Planned expansion of the size or number of facilities or relocation to larger quarters or a new market can mean business to you. Or maybe you see a gallery stagnating a bit and can

Handwritten data, maybe on file cards, is a database. A computer database could be considered a set of file cards, with each card being a **record** (a collection of information associated with a person or business or product). Each category of information is a **field**. Design your database to include the types of information you believe will be helpful in tracking and managing your business contracts. Depending on which software you use, you can carry a record to any length, or build smaller databases and link them by the **key field**. For example, one database could be client information; another could include product history, and the two could be linked by a key field assigned to both records.

Client	Address	City/State	ZIP	Phone	Product	Qty	Date	Action
The Gallery	222 1st	Sausalito, CA	94965	(415) 555-5555	Walnut Chest	12	12/96	8/97 for 97 holiday
Allen, Nancy	123 Elm	Cincinnati, OH	45207	(513) 565-5555	New Prospect			Mortar/Pestle?
Jones, J & J	146 What	San Diego, CA	92101	(619) 554-3333	Mortar/Pestle	1	6/96	New design
Best Gallery	134 Twit	Belmont, CT	06426	(860) 555-4321	Frames & Boxes	6,9	2/96	
Neat Things	456 Main St.	Midtown, MA	02113	(617) 222-6666	Mortar/Pestle	2	8/96	Has new design
Smith, Sara	43 5th Ave.	New York, NY	10012	(212) 444-4444	Mortar/Pestle	2	8/95	New design

You want a list of who bought mortar/pestles before 8/96. You plug in the parameters that will give you only those records that apply:
Select records where "Product" <u>contains</u> mortar and "Date" <u>is</u> < 8/96

Set up your report to include **client, telephone, quantity and date:**

Jones, J&J   (619) 554-3333   1   6/96
Smith, Sara   (212) 444-4444   2   8/95

You can also format your output for letters and mailing labels.

Sara Smith
43 5th Ave
New York, NY 10012

Sara Smith
43 5th Ave
New York, NY 10012

TABLE 8-3 Anatomy of a database

suggest a fresh look or approach to keep the storefront active. Don't hesitate to suggest and to work with them as you travel the sales road together.

INCREASING SALES

Whether growth is planned or brought on by success, you need a plan to meet the increased demand.

If you don't want to expand capacity, consider:

- Increasing prices—Find out if there is more upside in the pricing, and if wholesaling, negotiate more favorable commission rates, find new galleries or do more direct retail sales.
- Adding value to the product

If expansion is needed to increase output, look at:

- Adding more product—new designs, more variations, more units
- Finding more clients to buy more product
- Expanding into larger quarters
- Adding employees
- Taking on a partner
- Associating yourself with a promoter

To produce more quantity at equal or better quality (assuming you are producing your maximum), get help. This could be an apprentice (with you as the master craftsperson), a part-time helper, an independent contractor, or a full-time employee to help with production. Or get help in sales and marketing, office administration or wherever your attention is growing thin. Calculate how much time this would free for making product and whether that increased production time would cover the added expenses.

Know yourself—Some businesspeople weren't born to just maintain. Status quo is no challenge. You may want to expand, to try new products, new avenues, new ventures. Be what you want to be, do what you like to do. These are a few of the advantages of being an entrepreneur.

Do the obvious—Expand your market into more craft shows, trade shows, exhibitions.

Make yourself known—Use networking and publicity. Become a newsmaker by making yourself available and ready for media interest. Printed press releases, electronic media via fax, bulletin boards or your own home page on the World Wide Web all help in getting your name out to more prospective buyers.

Speaking of the Web, chapter two contains a primer on the Internet and how you can use it for locating resources. You can easily be one of those resources by building your own website for your business.

Sal Maccarone (see profile in chapter six) has done this and has linked himself to all sorts of related sites so a potential client can surf through architects and designers and be directed to Sal's page as a resource for custom furniture, sculpture and leaded glass to fill their new home. Try Sal's website (http://www.waypt.com/maccarone) to see how he approached the task.

If you're into this kind of thing, look into having this done for you. Many companies, many of which are home-based businesses, provide website design, Web hosting and programming. One local source quoted $100 for setup plus $10 per month for a single document with two images to $1000 for setup plus $100 a month for up to 20 documents, 240 images, custom response forms, domain registration and virtual server. To get more information and current, local pricing, use a provider in your area, or contact Liz Bartlett (http://www.idyllmtn.com/~khyri), or via more conventional means: Liz Bartlett, 110 E. Wilshire Ave. #G-10, Fullerton, CA 92832; telephone (714) 526-5656.

LESS "TECHIE" WAYS

You don't need the Web to increase your exposure. Get more involved in woodworker's guilds and co-ops that collectively hold exhibitions, and may run retail galleries and studios. Even service clubs, if you're so inclined, can be good network links. Another possibility, if you are feeling philanthropic, would be to donate one of your pieces to a fund-raiser. Charitable auctions, silent or otherwise, showcase your work to prominent prospects. Incidently, according to the IRS the cost of materials for donation is an allowable write-off (the cost of the labor is not).

NAME: **Michael Elkan**

LOCATION: **Silverton, Oregon**

PRODUCT: **Burl boxes, furniture, accessories**

SINCE: **1979**

TRAINING: **Self-taught**

SHOP: **Two buildings, 3000 sq. ft.**

PRICING: **90 percent wholesale**

AFFILIATIONS: **Regional/national market shows (ACC, The Rosen Group). Strong gallery presence (The Real Mother Goose, Portland, Oregon; Appalachian Springs, Washington, DC) Sterling Publishing Co., May 1996. Author of *Reading the Wood*.**

Michael Elkan came into woodworking from a business background, a product of the clothing industry. He coupled his later appreciation for woodworking with his desire to salvage unwanted, unsuitable items into a product.

Introduced as "the only woodworker in the business who drives a Jaguar," he counters, "People often pigeonhole me as 'Oh, he does well because he's a businessman. He knows business.' On the other hand, I think my true calling in the world is to find scrap and find a use for it. I think it is that more than anything else."

Q **What event launched your change to full-time woodworking?**

A I quit the clothing field when I was 30, leaving New Jersey in 1972. For seven years I was doing odd jobs and working on the place and doing some consulting in the clothing business. I didn't get into woodworking until 1979, when I started playing with wood by building a Morris Chair, then other smaller things. That same year, we went back east for a wedding, and I took some boxes along to test a few galleries. I showed them to George Nakashima, and he bought some to show in his gallery. And I hit a few other galleries with good results.

Q **Who or what was most helpful?**

A I couldn't name one person or one thing. My father was an incredible influence. Really it has been an accumulation of experiences. Nakashima was a great influence, as were Sam Maloof and Wharton Esherick, two of my favorite woodworkers. James Krenov was also a great influence. Even though his work is nothing like what I do, he read the wood. And the people, who over the years have said, "I love it!" or "You're an artist!"

Q **What was the most valuable skill or attribute you brought to the business?**

A I enjoy taking something useless and making it into something. I did it in the clothing business and continued it in what I do with wood.

Q **What obstacles did you encounter?**

A Many times just dealing with people, workers in particular. I've had the least amount of trouble working with galleries. Probably my own impatience. I find that the more you work a problem—a second time, a third time—the more frustrating it can be, and it never works out. I have found the best results are those that just happen. Instead of pushing and pushing a situation, it is sometimes better to go with the flow and to go on.

Q **What are your plans for growth?**

A In five years I hope the people that work with me can take over what I do. These people have been with me for eight to ten years and know what they are doing. I would continue to do the pieces I like to do. Although the majority of the output would no longer be signature pieces, they would still carry on the line.

I might do more writing (but I haven't been asked)—maybe about selecting wood for furniture. The concept of *Reading the Wood* was to be autobiographical, to encourage people from any background to succeed without necessarily going back to school, if they have the desire.

Q How do you sell your work?

A Primarily through galleries. Almost 99 percent of the work is sold outright. A small amount of work is consigned—furniture to one gallery. But even including furniture, most of it is sold. I wholesale my rocking chair and stools and a few other things.

Q What is your mix of sales of what you produce?

A There are actually four divisions in what I do. There is a mirror division, which includes hand mirrors, mirrored boxes and a vanity mirror. There is a dovetail group, which is a desk block, bookends and a clock/base combination piece and a dovetail box. Those are production items as we know it, but they are slightly different because we handpick every piece of wood. We don't just take a board and mark out a hundred mirrors. We read the wood and mark out the board as we see it. It could be a group of items from one board depending on how we see the board.

Furniture is the third division, and the fourth is the boxes, and even the boxes are split into two areas. We do what I call one-of-a-kind production boxes: a keeper or a hinged box, or a tall keeper or a natural jewelry box, and these are a style of box but there are no two alike. We don't use any templates to size the boxes. Each one is individual.

They're not the same size or the same height or the same thickness. And then there are the sculptural boxes, which are one-of-a-kind boxes.

Q So the one-of-a-kinds have some similarity to the next, but the sculptural boxes are free-form?

A Pretty much. Although even in there, we do some sort of sculptural pieces that are one-of-a-kind production. For instance, we might have a box that wholesales at $100. When we go to the shows we might get orders for 30 or 40 of them, and they may run from $80 to $125 to $150. There will be some similarities between the boxes, but again there are no templates used, so each one will be a different piece, designed and priced accordingly.

Q Of your galleries, do you seek out new outlets?

A We've been doing this for 17 years, so it is different from someone just starting out. We're showing in probably 200 to 250 galleries.

Q And are these found through shows such as the ACC?

A The American Craft Council shows and the Rosen shows. When I started back in 1979, that trip to the East Coast—we went back for a wedding—really gave me the push to go ahead and do what I do. On that first trip I went to about five or six different galleries and showed them what I was doing, and they bought them. That was a good indicator, and then I kind of knew what was happening.

Previous to that, when I very first started, the first place we showed the work was at the Oregon State Fair, where they had a courtyard they called the "craft courtyard," and it was one of the early venues for craft work. Judy Mullins, the communications person at the State Fair, started it around 1975, and it was kind of a hippie thing. I got in about 1979. The real indicator for me was that the work we did during that first summer sold out in the first few days. So it was then we decided that we'd better learn how to hop to it.

Q Is there one particular gallery that does the majority of your sales?

A The Real Mother Goose in Portland is my major gallery, which is one of the major players in the entire country. Another top one would be Appalachian Spring in Washington, DC. They are two of the top galleries. Appalachian Springs has been voted number one in the poll done by The Rosen Group for the past couple of years. The Real Mother Goose is right up there with them.

The Real Mother Goose gallery does a phenomenal job. I pretty much merchandise my work myself, so I can have a selection of my work there, and I can fill in or change the work as I see the need. That's an unusual situation, but it does allow me to be the merchandiser for the work. And, as long as the work produces, they're happy with it.

Q Part of that is nurturing your market?

A And they can't order ten boxes at $25 each. We don't price it that way because we make the work as the wood dictates. So I might make a certain amount of $25 boxes, $30 boxes and $35 and $40, $50 and $100 and $1000. Out of one batch of wood there will be everything we make coming out of the kiln load, even when it is all the same wood. So, when someone buys from us, the regular accounts rarely ask for a price. They'll just say, "Send me some keeper boxes, send me some hinge boxes, send me cave dweller type boxes," and we price the work to sell.

Q What is the overhead rate you try to attain?

A I don't work by an hourly rate. I don't even have a clue. I also think doing so is b---s---. If you make 50 boxes or 100 boxes, you don't know how to price your work. Some people will tell a crafts-

man that they're giving their time away. A mechanic makes $40 an hour and you're better than a mechanic so charge $40. So if you spend 40 hours making a chair, is it a $1600 chair at the wholesale level? Chances are it's not.

Pricing by the hour when starting out, you are charging prices you have no right to charge. In selling, there is a fair price for everything. You can sell one of anything at any price, but is it a fair value?

Q How would you rank quality, design, craftsmanship and pricing in their order of importance to the customer?

A I would hope—I don't know—that the first thing they feel is an emotion, and that emotion is a deciding factor in wanting the product and what they will pay for it. The object has to hit the customer first.

And they want something to last and expect the quality, design and craftsmanship. Pricing may come into play when a corporate buyer is looking for gift premiums.

Q Without divulging your gross income, what growth rate have you experienced?

A We hit a peak about 1991 in the volume of work, but since 1993, I've been making a conscious effort to do less business. I never wanted a big business. It was never my goal to have six employees. I had nine at one time but it was getting too big. So we have been trimming down. There was no problem hiring people to do the work, just more pressure. I decided I wanted a more manageable business.

Q How many people do you employ?

A We currently have five full-time woodworkers or artisans; two on mirror production and the others in sculpture and furniture. I also have an office manager who has been with us about three years. My brother started in that position from the beginning.

PROMOTERS AND MARKETING RESOURCES

A few of the artisans profiled here actively pursue outside sales support over and above what they personally can or care to handle. Some of the woodworking shows you may have considered may be marketing arms of craft promoters. These organizations have developed other aids and communications to help you bring your product to market.

American Craft Council

In addition to information on their various annual venues of ACC Craft Fairs, as a member of the American Craft Council you have their resources available for your use to be applied to your business needs. Membership does not guarantee you will be juried into a national show, but it will allow them to keep you abreast of upcoming events.

The ACC is divided into four units: American Craft Publishing, producing *American Craft* magazine; American Craft Enterprises—the for-profit arm of this nonprofit organization—which develops marketing opportunities for American craftspeople; the American Craft Information Center, which is a repository of a collection of craft-related publications; and American Craft Association (ACA), a trade and professional division of ACC catering to individuals and small businesses.

Member benefits include access to the ACC's library and database, free admission to ACC Craft Fairs on public days, and free admission to the American Craft Museum. Professional craftspeople get the above benefits, plus their newsletter, access to group health, property and casualty insurance, a listing in the ACC Crafts Registry database and more, for either $40 (ACC) or $50 (ACA) membership fees. The Council offers a variety of marketing, exhibition and member programs. Their mission, paraphrased, is to benefit American craft by educating the public through exhibits that showcase and market contemporary craft.

The American Craft Council Library's collection includes:

- craft registry and database: portfolios of 2500 juried craftspeople available for review at the library
- books: American craft
- exhibition catalogs: listing craft-related exhibitions
- periodicals
- craft organization file and database: local, regional and national newsletters of craft organizations, museums, galleries, shops and educational institutions
- archives: materials on ACC since its founding in 1943, and the American Craft Museum, founded as the Museum of Contemporary Crafts in 1956
- library guides: include business, careers and education in crafts, funding sources, locating craft shops, galleries, fairs and events, among other helpful topics

The Rosen Group, Wendy Rosen

You can also be taken under the wing of promoters, in addition to the above or exclusively. Promoters, such as The Rosen Group, provide marketing opportunities to help artists achieve success.

"Buyers Market of American Craft" is a semiannual event showcasing more than 2500 artisans to galleries and craft retailers throughout the country. 1996 Buyers Markets were held at the Pennsylvania Convention Center in Philadelphia.

The Rosen Group also hosts the Craft Business Institute in Baltimore each September. These workshops and seminars cover a wide range of topics including product development, pricing, public relations, accounting and wholesaling for craftspeople to hone their business skills for selling production, limited production and one-of-a-kind work. See chapter seven for periodicals that the Rosen Group publishes.

Ohio Designer Craftsmen Guild

Chartered to serve Ohio craftspeople, the ODCG operates the Ohio Craft Museum in Columbus, Ohio, holds two statewide meetings per year, and has an exhibition program and newsletter. NOTE: Participation in the Guild is for a certain locale, per their charter;

other organizations may be operating in your area.

Ohio Design Craftsman Enterprises, a for-profit arm of the Ohio Design Craftsmen, owns and operates four retail galleries in Ohio (one each in Cleveland and Cincinnati and two in Columbus) under the name A Show of Hands to develop marketing opportunities for Ohio craftspeople through their retail studios.

Each store keeps a slide file of guild members' work, and the Ohio Guild publishes an annual catalog of work from the artisans. This catalog is made available to other galleries, interior designers, architects and buyers of corporate premiums. ODC Enterprises represents member craftspeople at major shows, such as The Rosen Group's Buyers Market show in Philadelphia twice each year and the George Little International Gift Show in New York.

The ODCG also publishes a wholesale buyer's resource directory, which is open nationally, under the title of *Lifestyle Crafts*. Twice yearly, they mail about 20,000 to qualified store buyers. These generate 12,000 responses each issue. The artisan receives these customer inquiry cards and even pressure-sensitive labels to use on replies. Marketing advice in the form of a reminder to follow up by telephone helps the ODCG member conduct business. Membership also entitles the craftsperson to a marketing consultation. In addition to the $25 membership fee, *Lifestyle Crafts* offers advertising space to qualified artisans. As of this writing, the fee was $490 for a quarter-page illustrated ad.

Jonathan Simons, of Jonathan's Spoons (see profile in chapter seven), avails himself of the many services of the American Craft Council and The Rosen Group, advertising in *NICHE* magazine, and his ads also appear in the Ohio Design Craftsmen Guild *Lifestyle Crafts*, among others. His products are well suited to a broader marketing approach.

GETTING INTO GALLERIES AND ENTERING SHOWS

Christopher Brooks's credentials have earned him a spot as a juror for both national and regional shows. A few of his thoughts on the process and roadblocks to breaking into these shows may help the novice or encourage previously rejected craftspeople to try again if these shows fit their objectives.

According to Brooks, the number of entrants vying for an opportunity to show their work can be overwhelming for the jury panel. Even in nonjuried shows, about 300 artists might be reviewed in a session, and there is no specific order in which they appear on the docket. Furniture can be followed by a dulcimer, mirrors and toys, so it is sometimes difficult to rank pieces within a product in any order. How does the desk you see late in the afternoon compare with the one you accepted, or maybe rejected, early in the morning?

Photo quality

Make your first slide a grabber. There are so many entrants to review that the panel might not get past the first of a number of entries submitted by an artisan. Select the best of the best to elicit interest. The first slide must be a zinger, a photographic hand that grabs the jurors by their collective lapels and says, "Look at me!"

A dramatic, clear photo of the piece you are entering must make the style, proportions, details and finish obvious in the first few seconds on the screen. If the first slide is unimpressive, any additional slides of this or your accompanying entries may go unreviewed.

The American Craft Council has adopted a format to eliminate the problem of sequence. Show registration kits contain a card for viewing in a five-projector montage projected simultaneously on a single screen.

The quality of your slides showing the work, or type of work, you propose, submitted for entry is important. When they are all shown at once, the total presentation needs to be the grabber. Professional studio shots, although not required, may help. If you take them yourself, remove any clutter, place the piece in a complementing setting or on a seamless backdrop, and maybe use some floodlights for flattering illumination. When shooting color film, cut the fluorescent light or use a red filter to remove the green cast given off by fluorescent lighting.

Do you really need a photo studio setup? You might

if you intend to document your work, to build your portfolio, or maybe to submit a few ideas to Betterway Books, Taunton Press, Sterling Publications, etc. The setup can be relatively inexpensive if you already have the camera equipment. Studio lighting can be as simple as a couple of floodlights clipped to the rafters.

Selection process

Selection committees for various types of shows and exhibitions, and even galleries, are diverse. For ACC shows, the jury gives craftspeople who participate in its events the opportunity to elect selection committees. Each media category has a committee of six craftspeople who work in the medium and three wholesale buyers, and these committees determine what will be exhibited in the events.

Local festivals, such as the Laguna Festival of the Arts, fill 165 artist spaces each summer, drawing from local artisans. This is a juried system for maybe 25 to 35 openings that are created by tenured artists on sabbatical or juried out. The Board selects the jury, comprised of four current exhibitors plus three jurors from outside the community. These are selected for a balance of contemporary and traditional art and craft mediums and photography.

Nonjuried shows, festivals and fairs are handled similarly. For A Show of Hands, the ODCG board members meet monthly to review new work being presented for representation. While the level of competition is not as great as that for national shows, the work needs to meet their criteria for originality, design, quality and craftsmanship. Since the number of competitors is far smaller (six to ten per month, compared with the hundreds of entries for a major national show), the presentation may be a little less polished.

Craftspeople known to the Guild can mention a new item and be invited in. Those not yet known have to go an extra step in making a good first impression, so something more than a quick snapshot or color copy of the work would give the applicant an edge. What they look for in new work is design, size, price and delivery. They may use one of their stores to test market a new product or artist. Each of the stores focuses on one artist each month, which can include some consigned pieces that may not be part of the normal inventory. Items selected for retailing are bought outright at the craftsperson's wholesale price.

DERIVATIVES

During start-up, you were probably forced to work in areas that were not directly aligned to your creative objectives. This activity kept food on the table and elicited a following in what you want to make. These offshoots can serve you in the growth phase as well. After experiencing the reality of fulfilling your objectives, you might have found a new interest, a new direction that promotes your growth and interest in the business.

Maybe you have found a strong marketing bent and want to represent other artisans to their customers or to galleries. Or you can gather a few well-suited talents to form a craft center or a co-op venture, an association within the brick and mortar of a village craft site or a site in cyberspace.

A manufacturing interest can completely change the scope and nature of your original wood crafting interests. The transition can come about by design or by demand; one day you might find yourself at a desk rather than a saw.

Collecting, appraising and consulting on furniture and craft are other areas where you could direct your talents.

Retailers of woodworking materials, tools and equipment are always looking for sales representatives who know woodworking and can help customers with their supply needs. The industry sells to 18+ million woodworkers, from hobbyists to professionals, who spend $7 billion annually to support this habit.

Publishing or writing is another tangent that promotes a skill, a sector or a movement. Video production, website design, or even your own *This Old Furniture* syndicated show are options. You could become the expert and be a reviewer of new titles, or become a publicist for the artisans and craftspeople of the day.

INDEX